SUCCESSFUL
Sunday School
TEACHING

D0926314

by

MYER PEARLMAN

GOSPEL PUBLISHING HOUSE
Springfield, Missouri 65802

2-606

[PRINTED
IN U·S·A]

Contents

Foreword

The purpose of this book is to set forth in simple language the most important principles governing teaching, and Sunday School teaching in particular. Technical terms have been carefully avoided in order to make the book helpful primarily to those Sunday School teachers who may have had little or no previous training in the art of teaching. The subject has been treated in a general way to make it adaptable, as far as possible, to the use of teachers of all departments of the Sunday School.

1

The Teacher's Task

He who has responded to the call to teach a Sunday School class has indeed chosen a great work, for his call carries with it the privilege and responsibility of co-operating with God in the molding of Christian character and the imparting of spiritual knowledge. In a very real sense he has been called to the ministry. Recognizing the importance and dignity of his calling, he will determine by God's help to attain the highest possible efficiency in his work, making it a real vocation.

First of all he will seek for that which cannot be acquired by mere study; namely, those spiritual gifts peculiarly suitable to the teacher. 1 Cor. 12:7-10, 28. Then, remembering that God always works in co-operation with our intelligent efforts, he will begin his self-preparation by asking the following questions:

Why shall I teach, or, what is my purpose and motive? He must have a clear-cut perception of his main aim in teaching; he must know what he is "driving at," otherwise, if his aim is vague, so will be the results of his teaching. After considering the matter carefully, the truly spiritual teacher will conclude that his chief work and the end of all his efforts will be the employing of the truths of the Bible to lead his students to an experimental knowledge of Christ, so that every lesson shall be an instrument skillfully used for the production and training of Christian character. In brief, his main objective will be a spiritual one.

Whom shall I teach, or, what class of students will be the subjects of my teaching? The teacher's gifts and qualifications will soon reveal whether he is suited best to the teaching of adults, young people, intermediates, juniors, primaries, or beginners.

What shall I teach, or, what knowledge of my subject do I possess? The main subject of his teaching will of course be the Bible; therefore he should do all within his power to master its history, doctrines, geography, and customs. "Thou therefore which teachest another, teachest thou not thyself?" Rom. 2:21. The teacher cannot impart what he does not know, he cannot explain what he does not understand, nor can he speak with authority unless he has mastered his subject. The person who intends to make a "job" of teaching will study "without ceasing," will be a diligent reader along all lines of Biblical knowledge, and will perhaps take up some systematic study of the Word. This program most certainly involves hard work, but one does not slide into effective and efficient teaching ability. The real teacher must earn the bread of a fruitful teaching ministry with the sweat of his brow. However, all hard effort will pay rich returns.

How shall I teach? This is a very important question to be answered; for no matter how much knowledge a teacher may possess, he will fail if he does not know how to convey that knowledge to the minds of his students. And this question leads us to the subject of this book, which is, The How or the Art of Teaching Sunday School Lessons.

"Can one really learn how to teach? I thought that teaching was a gift that came to one naturally," we may imagine the reader saying. It is true that certain individuals possess a special aptitude for teaching, and it is also true that the art may be acquired. Some may appear to be "geniuses" along this line, but in most cases their genius is the result of two per cent inspiration and ninety-eight per cent perspiration, as Edison once said.

Teaching is an art that may be acquired because it is governed by definite laws. Let a person study and master those laws, and patiently and constantly apply them, and he will discover that he is "putting his lesson across." Success in teaching depends upon "knowing how."

2

What Is Teaching?

What is teaching? It is not merely telling facts, for the student may fail to understand, or may be inattentive; neither is it listening to recitations, which may simply be memorized and repeated in parrot-like fashion. Teaching may be defined as the arousing of the mind of a pupil to grasp and hold a certain truth. It is more than the mere imparting of truths to others; it is moving them to think out those facts for themselves.

To accomplish the purpose set forth in this definition, it is necessary to follow four principles which are the very foundation of teaching, and which comprise all the rules relating to teaching, stating in the simplest, clearest way the fundamental methods and purposes of teaching; in other words, if one is to teach correctly and effectively, four things must be done:

First, the teacher must get the student to think for himself, use his own ideas, come to his own conclusions, and in general, learn to do his own studying and discovering of truth. What is the meaning of the word "educate"? Literally, it means to "draw out" by question and suggestion what is in the student's mind, and those activities of which he is capable; in other words, education does not manufacture the engine—it sets it going. The most effective teacher is the one who captures the student's attention, arouses

8

his mind, creates interest and desire for knowledge, and then sets before him the material from which he may form his own conclusions. Teaching is not a matter of loading the mind with facts as a furnace is loaded with coal; it is a matter of supplying the raw material of question, suggestion, and necessary facts and of starting the machinery of the mind so that it turns out the finished product of well-reasoned-out thought. "Learning is self-teaching." An experienced teacher writes, "You must allow this instinct free play in your pupils. Do not thrust truth at them as if it were propaganda, but rather cover it up a little and only lead them near enough to see it, so that they may have the pleasure of lifting the veil themselves. Let them discover it in their own way. Let them even think that they are discovering it in spite of you. This will not hurt your feelings, for your business is to make them think, not how wonderful you are, but how wonderful truth is. Your most triumphant moment must be when some pupil comes to you to tell you about a great discovery that he has made, and you realize that it is just the thing that you have wanted him to learn. . . . The crowning glory of teaching is the ability to make the pupil feel that he is teaching you, rather than that you are teaching him. . . . Very likely you yourself can recall some teacher of your youth who stood modestly by while you rushed headlong into a new mansion of truth through a door which she held silently open for you."

Second, he must explain new truths by truths that the student already understands. Teaching is explaining the new by the old, the unknown by the known, the difficult by the simple, the obscure by the clear. And that is the *only* way to cause people to understand; for every new truth must be interpreted by the material already in their minds. For example, I say to the class, "How many have heard of the Chasidim?" My question is met by blank looks, for the listeners do not know whether "Chasidim" is a political party, a disease, or a new kind of breakfast food. The thought is entirely new, and conveys no image to the mind. But supposing I explain that "Chasidim" is the name of a Jewish sect living in central Europe. They believe in the outward operation of the Holy Spirit and maintain that religion should be more vital and emotional than that found among the other Jews. Because of their profession of a higher standard we might describe them as a "holiness movement" in the Jewish church. Do the listeners now understand who the Chasidim are? Why? Because I have used ideas and terms with which they are familiar, so that they have used their own minds to explain the word. The foreign-sounding word is no longer a stranger; it has been introduced by the teacher to some familiar residents in the student's mind. Again, suppose that we desire to teach a child of five an idea of the shape of the earth. Would it help him to understand if we should say, "The earth is spherical in shape"? Certainly not, for that would be an explanation requiring an explanation. On the other hand, if we explain that the earth upon which we live is a great, big round thing like an orange, he will be almost sure to grasp the idea. For we have explained something unknown to him by the use of a truth already familiar to him. To sum up: the efficient teacher will make it his business to know those ideas familiar to his pupils and will use them to enable his pupils to grasp new ideas.

Third, he must adapt the material to the age, understanding, and condition of his pupils. For example, in teaching a beginners' class the instructor will not speak of "regeneration," "sanctification," "predestination," or "pre-tribulation rapture." No, he will impart the truths implied by those theological terms in a form that can be digested by the minds of children. Note how Paul, the apostle, employed this principle. He had but one gospel for Jew and Gentile; but study his sermons in the book of Acts, and you will notice that he served the divine food in one way to Jews and in another to the Gentiles. In the one instance he connected the gospel with the Old Testament doctrines, which the Jews understood; in the other, he connected it with the Book of Nature which the Gentiles understood. The real teacher will understand the peculiarities, interests, and ways of thinking which belong to the stage of growth of his pupils, and will adapt his teaching accordingly. A radio announcer will adjust his microphone according to the height of the speaker. If the former speaker was six feet tall and the next speaker is only five feet tall the announcer will lower the microphone. A great part of the teacher's skill consists in knowing how to adjust the spiritual teachings to the spiritual stature of his listeners.

Fourth, he will strive to connect one lesson with another, truth with truth, doctrine with doctrine, incident with incident, in order to organize within the student's mind a unified knowledge of Bible history and doctrine. His task is not to deliver so many portions of knowledge in order to create a store of information in the student's mind; rather his task each Sunday will be to conduct intelligently the erection of a symmetrical structure of Christian character and Christian knowledge. And, in order to do this, it will be necessary for him to possess the "blueprints," so to speak, in order that he may work intelligently and systematically to that end. He must ascend, figuratively speaking, into the mount of prayer and study, there to receive the pattern for the construction of the tabernacle of character and knowledge, so that, like Moses, he may hear the voice of God admonishing him, "See that thou make all things according to the pattern shewed to thee in the mount." Heb. 8:5. Let us illustrate this principle by imagining that the series of lessons for the quarter covers the life of Christ. The teacher is about to begin a lesson. At a certain point in the introduction he will say, "This morning we are to study the Sermon on the Mount, which sets forth the laws of the Kingdom. Let us look back and see how far we have proceeded in the story of the King. In our first lesson we considered *the earthly descent and heavenly nature of the King;* in the next lesson we were told *how the King was first received* by different classes; next, we were given a description of the great prophet who acted as the *herald of the King;* then, in the next lesson of the Baptism and Temptation of Jesus we witnessed the *public presentation and private preparation of the King* before His active ministry; in the lesson following we studied about the *King's first exercise of authority* in the calling of His first followers, or ministers in His kingdom. In our lesson for today we shall listen to the *King's proclamation of the laws of His king-*

dom, and next Sunday we shall consider *the power*
to the *King's proclamation of the laws of His king-*
kingdom."

Notice what the teacher has done. Instead of
presenting the Sermon on the Mount as an isolated
portion of Scripture, he has set it forth as a vital
part of the life and ministry of Christ. In other
words, he is using the quarter's lesson on the life of
Christ as a means of building up within the student's
mind a connected outline of the life of Christ.

Let us take another example. The class is studying the second chapter of the Gospel according to
Matthew. The teacher says, "We see that Herod the
Great, a wicked king, was incited by Satan to kill all
the children of Bethlehem, in order that he might
destroy God's King and our Redeemer. But God
spoiled his plan. Now, think back in Old Testament
history for a moment, and call to mind that incident
which relates how a babe, who was to be Israel's deliverer, escaped the power of a wicked ruler who had
decreed that the male children among the Israelites
should be slain." And many in the class will remember the childhood of Moses and will notice the re-
semblance in the experiences of the Mediator of the
Old Covenant and the Mediator of the New Covenant.
The teacher continues: "In this same chapter Matthew
tells us that the Messiah, when a child, was sent to
Egypt for protection before proceeding to Palestine,
where He was to serve God and His people. Is there
anything in this that reminds you of an Old Testament
incident?" And very likely some in the class will remember that when Israel was a young nation God sent
them down to Egypt for preservation, and then sent

them to the Holy Land, there to serve Him. Compare Ex. 4:22 and Matt. 2:15. Notice again what the teacher has done: he has connected Old and New Testament history in such a way as to make the student understand that there is a real connection between them; that they are part of one Divine plan; and that many of the Old Testament incidents are prophetic types of Christ's life, work, and ministry.

Let us further apply this principle. The lesson, let us say, is based upon the incident of Christ's feeding the multitude. The teacher says, "Christ fed the multitude in the wilderness. Of what Old Testament event does that remind you?" Someone will answer, "Moses' feeding the Israelites with manna in the wilderness." The teacher then remarks, "That would lead many of the Jews to look upon Christ as a second Moses, as a God-sent Deliverer to Israel, would it not?" Thus the teacher has made a *historical* connection. He continues: "God, through Moses, fed the Israelites with supernatural food in the wilderness; Christ likewise fed the hungry in the wilderness. Is it not true then that in a sense, because the world in which we live is a wilderness to the spiritual life, that we still need the bread that comes from heaven?" He has made a *spiritual* connection. He proceeds: "Can you think of the sacred service which reminds us that we are in continual need of spiritual nourishment to sustain our spiritual life in this world, and that Jesus alone, the Bread of life, can sustain us?" And the answer will naturally be, "The Communion service." The teacher has made a *doctrinal* connection. He continues: "If we are deprived of natural food we become hungry, and if the deprivation continues, or the food is scant, we become undernourished and sick. In like manner when we neglect spiritual nourishment, when we fail to pray and read the Word, we become spiritually hungry, undernourished, and weak." The teacher has made a *personal* connection. Once again: "The world is full of people who are spiritually hungry and who are burdened with sin, sickness, and sorrow. Christ can feed and satisfy them. However, we have a responsibility in the matter, for He says to us, as He said to His disciples, 'Give ye them to eat.' " The teacher has thus made a *practical* connection by relating the lesson to the Christian's missionary responsibility.

To sum up: the teacher must be constantly connecting the various portions of the Scriptures—connecting history with doctrine, prophecy with fulfillment, book with book, Old Testament with New, type with antitype; so that the pupil learns that the Bible is not a mere collection of texts and incidents, but a living unity, the parts of which are as vitally related to one another as the members of the human body. And, as we shall see later, he must be constantly connecting the lesson with life, so that the pupil will not place its teaching in a water-tight compartment of his mind and so separate it from his daily life.

3

Methods of Teaching

A noted scholar once wrote: "Before a speaker faces his audience, he should write to his friend and say, 'I am going to make an address on a subject, and I want to make these points.' He should enumerate the things that he is going to speak about in their correct order. If he finds that he has nothing to say in his letter, he had better write to the committee that invited him and say that the possible death of his grandmother will probably prevent his being present on the occasion."

This is a rather humorous way of telling us that we have no business addressing an audience without adequate preparation on our part. And the admonition certainly applies to Sunday School teaching. A well prepared lesson is nine-tenths delivered. And a well-prepared lesson includes, not only the knowledge of *what* to teach, but also of *how* to teach. Assuming that the teacher is well supplied with material, he must ask himself this question: "How shall I deliver these truths to the class? Shall I do all the talking, or shall I ask questions and let them do the work?" In other words, "What method shall I use?"

There are many methods of presenting a lesson, just as there are many ways of delivering goods to a customer. For example, one may go in person to deliver the goods; or, he may call up the customer and ask him to call for them. The particular method used will depend upon the nature of the class, the ability of the teacher, and other circumstances. For the sake of convenience we shall classify the methods according to the following divisions: (1) methods that throw the burden of the work upon the teacher; (2) methods that lay a large part of the burden upon the class; (3) and methods in which teacher and class co-operate.

1. THE TEACHER AT WORK

In the following two methods the burden of work falls on the teacher.

The Lecture Method. In this method the teacher presents the lesson very much in the same manner as the preacher delivers his sermon; he does the talking, while the class does the listening. It has its advantages: it gives the teacher the entire time of the lesson period in which to present the lesson, in a thorough, definite, and systematic manner, to a group of busy people who cannot, or will not, find time to prepare their lesson. This method would be necessary where the class is so large that recitation or discussion would interfere with the adequate presentation of the lesson. It is understood, of course, that one who uses the lecture method should be an able and forceful speaker, who can hold the attention and interest of the class; otherwise some may go "woolgathering" and others may doze. This method has its weakness in that it does not sufficiently stimulate the student to activity in the way of lesson preparation.

The Narrative Method. In the lower departments the entire lesson consists in the telling of a story, for that is the form in which spiritual truth can best be assimilated by the minds of children. In the higher departments this method can, and should, be used when the lesson centers around a Biblical incident, for a well-told story is a sure method of securing and holding attention. Every teacher should cultivate the art of story-telling; he should be able to project himself into Biblical times, see the scenes, walk with the people, hear their conversation, understand their customs, and then describe vividly what he sees. In this manner Bible history becomes "real" to his listeners. And even in doctrinal lessons, when the lesson cannot be presented in story form, the teacher may brighten the lesson with well-pointed illustrations, and stories skillfully told. If he realizes that he has led the class into a dry desert of uninteresting exposition, he may save the day and regain their interest by quickly finding an oasis in the form of an interesting illustration connected with the lesson.

2. THE PUPIL AT WORK

We have noticed that one of the fundamental tasks of the teacher is to get the pupil to do his own thinking. He will refrain, therefore, from telling the student what he can find out for himself. One of the best methods for realizing the principle of self-activity is the one which may be described as the *recitation method*. After the teaching period, the teacher devotes a little time to an assignment for the next lesson. He assigns a certain task to each student; to one, the working out of some questions; to another, the development of a certain topic; to another, the drawing of a map, etc. This procedure has a good psychological effect upon the student; it makes him feel that the teacher means business and knows his business; and further, it gives the joy of the accomplishment of a task.

"But how shall I get the pupil to study?" This is a question that naturally arises from the consideration of this method. We would make the following suggestions:

Show him how to study. Very likely he does not know how to go about the work. And one of the most useful lessons a person can learn in any school is how to study for himself.

"Do not just tell them how and let it go at that," advises Mr. Suter in his book, *Creative Teaching* (Macmillan Co.). "Show them how. In the early part of the school year it will probably pay to take at least half, if not whole, lesson periods for exercises with this aim. Gather your pupils around you and say, 'Now I am going to pretend that I am one of you, and I am going to study and prepare a lesson.' Then go through the actual process, step by step, leaving out nothing. Use every book and leaflet, paper or notebook, exactly as the pupil would do. When it comes to reading the assigned passages read out loud (this will be the only difference between what you do and what the pupil does at home.) When it comes to writing do the actual writing. In other words, give a perfect demonstration and explain as you go the reasons for doing the different things and the best way of doing each."

A nationally known Sunday School writer and teacher of long experience, Amos R. Wells, tells us one of the things he would do if he had his work to do over again: "If I had it to do over again I should think less of what I was giving and more of what they were getting. I did little or nothing at the start, to make my pupils study at home. I gave out no home work. My teaching was all lectures, though usually under the thin disguise of questions and answers. Thus I was all the time pouring into a basket full of holes. Their home study, though probably it would have been very inadequate, yet would have provided a solid cup of attention into which I might have poured something that they would have retained."

Inspire his interest and give him a motive for study. If we wish to persuade a person to perform a task we must make him feel that it is worth while, that the mastering of the lesson will really do something for him. The teacher, like a salesman, must create a desire for his product.

Instead of assigning in a general way to the class at large, *assign a definite task to each individual* and hold him responsible for it.

Do your best to call for recitation of each piece of work assigned; otherwise the students will become negligent, and say, "What's the use of studying? We are not called upon to recite anyway."

"But won't the lesson become rather dry if it consists only of the recitation of the pupils?" is another question that will arise in connection with this method. It will, if the lesson is limited to the students' recitation. But it becomes the teacher's task to "fill in" between the answers and so develop the lesson in an interesting way. If we compare the assignment of the lesson to orders for the construction of various sections of a house, we may compare the teacher's work to the assembling of that house and the displaying of the finished product. As each answer is given, each recitation made, the teacher will complete, comment upon, and, if necessary, correct it, and then weave it into the developing lesson.

3. TEACHER AND STUDENT WORKING TOGETHER

The Question Method. In this method the teacher stimulates the thoughts of the class by the use of skillful questions that set them thinking. In a real sense he "educates" the class by drawing from their own minds the main facts of the lesson. This is one of the most interesting of methods, for it keeps the listeners alert and active. And it helps the teacher, too, by taking from his shoulders the burden of lecturing; his position becomes that of a foreman directing the erection of a building.

But the method has its dangers. The students may neglect to study the lesson, and where there is no previous preparation the answers may tend to become superficial and a matter of guess-work. Then too, there is a danger of spending too much time discussing some minor detail, or some question not connected with the lesson, thus wandering from the main point. It then becomes the teacher's task to keep the discussion to the point, and tactfully to prevent discussion of side-issues or irrelevant matters.

The Question-Recitation Method is a combination of the recitation and interrogative methods. The teacher makes a definite assignment, and then develops the lesson by a discussion in which he calls upon each student to give the results of his study. Providing the class is of the right size, and the students can be induced to study, this is the most effective method. Otherwise, for adult classes, the question method is the most interesting.

4

Mastering the Lesson

Our lesson text and quarterly are before us. How shall we master the material? Let us consider the following suggestions.

Begin early and study daily. It is an excellent plan to set apart a certain portion of time—say a half hour every day—for the preparation of next Sunday's lesson; and if one finds it possible to observe the same period each day, so much the better, for a regular habit will thus be developed. Why begin early? An early start gives time for thorough study and medita· tion, so that the lesson penetrates into mind and heart, and becomes, as it were, a part of us. We are all familiar with the children's game of rolling a snow-ball along the snow-covered ground until it assumes large proportions. In like manner truths of the lesson may develop in our minds as we turn them round and round in the process of study and meditation.

This is what takes place when we begin the study of the lesson early in the week. We spend, say, a half hour surveying the lesson on Monday. The next day we shall discover that, though we may not have been aware of the fact, the mind has been working up-on the material so that it is clearer and better arranged. Further, during the day, flashes of truths will come to us as we go about our daily tasks—an illustration, a reference, something we may read in a book, a lum-inous thought, etc. And when we sit down to the lesson on Tuesday evening the lesson text is no longer strange to us. Now let us imagine that we are confronted this evening with puzzling problems and questions over which we labor in vain, and which we leave in discouragement perhaps. We need not be disheartened, for probably the next day those truths may have been clarified through meditation, and we may see them in a new light. Thus we see, that aside from the advantage that comes from daily study, we are helped by a law known as the law of "unconscious cerebration," from which we learn that after hard, conscious study of a question, the mind will continue to work on it even while the person may be thinking over other matters. The well known practice of "sleeping over" a decision or problem is an example of this. But above all, through prayer, let us remember, it is possible for the teacher's mental faculties to be supernaturally stimulated. "He shall lead you into all truth," promised Christ. Note that the word "lead" implies that we shall be seeking the truth; in other words, studying.

What an able teacher said about the preparation of a speech may well be applied to the preparation of a lesson: "Determine your subject a week in advance, so that you will have time to think it over for seven nights. Think of it the last thing before you retire. Think of it the next morning while you are shaving, while you are bathing, while you are riding down town, while you are waiting for elevators, for lunch, for appointments. Discuss it with your friends. Make it a topic of conversation. Ask yourself all the possible questions concerning it."

To sum up: let us remember the "snowball" process and get the "ball a-rolling" early in the week.

Study thoroughly. "The Teacher at the Grindstone," is the title of one of the chapters in Marion Lawrance's book, *My Message to Sunday School Workers* (Richard R. Smith Co.), a helpful work by a Sunday School statesman. It well describes the necessary attitude of one who would be a successful Sunday School teacher. This same writer remarks: "It is said that eight pounds of steel will make an axe, but eight pounds of steel is not an axe. It requires three things—shape, edge, and polish. Preparation does this for a Sunday School teacher. Time spent at the grindstone makes the work easier. The teacher is the hinge upon which the Sunday School swings, and if the teacher is trained, then the hinge is oiled, and the work is apt to go more smoothly." Let us notice some suggestions for the teacher's study:

Study the lesson text for yourself before reading the quarterly; in fact, act as if you had no quarterly to help you. It is said that when ambitious students came to Agassiz, the great naturalist, he gave each a textbook on Natural Science?—no, he gave each a fish and told him to find out what he could about it. They went to work and in a day or two were ready for their report. But Agassiz did not come around. To kill time they went to work; they observed, dissected, conjectured, and at the end of a fortnight, when Agassiz finally appeared, they felt that their knowledge was really exhaustive. But the master's brief comment was that they had made a beginning, and again he left them. They continued their research and after weeks and months of investigation declared that a fish was the most fascinating of studies. Now, although most of us lack time to put such an amount of work and investigation into each lesson, we may derive the following lesson from this scientist's method: the best thoughts—the thoughts that "go over" with the greatest force—are those that have been forged in the fires of our own meditations and beaten out on the anvil of our own experience. And it is after we have worked hard on a lesson for ourselves that the quarterly becomes most valuable to us, for we approach it prepared. Of what use then is the quarterly? It will help us to arrange in systematic form the material that we have worked out for ourselves; it will explain details that seem obscure to us; it will supply us with new thoughts and with illustrations.

Gather more material than you really need in your lesson. The World War was fought not only by the soldiers on the front line, but also by those behind the lines. It is a fact that for every man in the frontline trenches there were at least ten men to support him—reserves, supply men, medical men, engineers, etc. In like manner, the material for the forty-minute lesson should be supported by several times more material than the teacher needs, for the possession of the "surplus capital" gives force to every word he speaks and imparts confidence to the class. What Dr. Dale Carnegie wrote about the preparation of a speech applies also to the preparation of a Sunday School lesson: "Collect more material, more information, than there is any possibility of employing. Get it for the additional confidence it will give you, for the sureness of touch. Get it for the effect that it will have upon your mind and heart and whole manner of speaking. 'I have drilled hundreds of salesmen, canvassers, and demonstrators,' says Arthur Dunn, 'and the principal weakness which I have discovered in most of them has been their failure to realize the importance of knowing everything possible about their products, and getting such knowledge before they start to sell.'" Sunday School teachers, speaking figuratively, are salesmen of the spiritual products of God's kingdom; they therefore should master the catalogue of the kingdom—the Bible—in which are listed the heavenly goods and values of the spiritual life.

Study the background of the lesson. If, for example, the lesson is from the Epistle to the Galatians, study the entire epistle; if you are to begin a series on one of the Gospels, it would be an excellent plan to read the entire Gospel through first; if the lesson deals with one of the incidents of the life of Josiah, one should study all the chapters in Kings and Chronicles dealing with his reign and also those prophecies in Jeremiah and Zephaniah that were uttered during that period. But why go to all this trouble? Because, the more we know about the *whole,* the clearer we can understand the *section.* To illustrate: a person who decides to become a heart specialist enters a medical college. Does he first of all begin the study of the heart? No; he is given a series of lessons on the human body as a whole, and on all of its parts and organs. Logically so; for the heart is so intimately connected with the rest of the body that its functions and disorders cannot be properly understood without a knowledge of the other organs. The medical student must *generalize* before he *specializes.* To apply the principle: the more a teacher knows about the Bible as a whole the better able he will be to expound one of its sections.

At this point the question will probably arise, How shall I gain this background knowledge? And this leads to the question of teacher-training. The efficient Sunday School teacher should seek to acquire the following Biblical knowledge: a knowledge of Scriptural history from Genesis to Revelation; a knowledge of the purpose and contents of each book of the Bible, in order that he may know where to find his material; the Life of Christ and the Life of Paul; the doctrines of the Bible; a knowledge of Biblical geography and customs. How shall one secure such knowledge? (1) The best method is to attend a teacher-training class if such can be organized and conducted in the local church. (2) One may take a correspondence course. (3) The teacher may secure some excellent books on the needed subjects and take a reading course.

Write out the results of your study as an aid to memory and as a means to getting the subject clearly in mind. We shall enlarge upon this topic in a later chapter.

Prepare prayerfully. The Sunday School teacher's main objective is not intellectual, but spiritual— the development of Christian character in his students. Therefore to impart spiritual knowledge successfully without the spiritual power that comes from prayer would be like trying to play a pipe organ with the electricity turned off. The necessity of prayer in the preparation of every lesson has been well stated by Mr. Suter. While what he says applies particularly to a class of boys, the general principle is true of all classes.

"In the course of a year you are allowed to make thirty-five impressions on these boys. (In our Sunday Schools where classes meet every Sunday of the year the number of such impressions would be fifty-two.) As a Christian warrior, the Sword of the Spirit, which is the Word of God, is placed in your hands, and the Church bids you wield thirty-five strokes for the kingdom of God. Each time you meet your class is a crisis. It is an experience for the boys which is so rare as to be almost unique. Everything depends upon how you acquit yourself, how you conduct the class. If you do nobly, you will put into the lives of the boys the impetus of thirty-five impulses toward loyalty to Christ. You will bring their souls into touch with a power which in the day of trial may just save them from calamity.

"On the other hand, if you manage your class badly through lack of preparation, if you stumble aimlessly through the forty minutes, if your work lacks purpose and intelligence and you lack poise, if you are nervous or distracted, or even only lazy and vague, you will not only lose your opportunity, but, worse still, you may do positive harm. I mean that by your carelessness and poor workmanship you will say to them in deeds that speak louder than words, that the whole enterprise known as the Christian religion is of so little account that it does not win the enthusiasm and kindle the best efforts of an adult who teaches it.

"You cannot 'turn off' your influence on a given Sunday because you do not feel up to your task, for whenever people meet together the forces of influence are brought into play even if no words are spoken. Influence them next Sunday you must, whether you wish to or not. The only question is whether you will influence them in the direction of Christlikeness or in some other direction. Therefore you must be sure that you are fit. You cannot do this work without God's help."

Prepare yourself. What has been said about prayer leads us to the thought that in Sunday School teaching the teacher is more important than the lesson itself, the worker more important than the work. Emerson has said, "Let me select the teacher, and I care not who selects the course of study." It is the life of the teacher that gives force to his teaching; what he *is* influences the class more forcibly than what he says. "Use what language you will," said the same writer, "you can never say anything but what you are." The teacher should ask himself, "Am I an example of the truth I am trying to give to the scholars? I am attempting to teach them to be patient; am I patient? I am endeavoring to teach them to pray; do I pray?" And it was on this principle that a man who was asked to address a group of teachers on the subject of "Behavior" spoke about the behavior of teachers and officers, rather than that of the pupils. What the cannon is to the shot, what the bow is to the arrow, so the teacher is to the lesson.

What has been said in this chapter may be well summed up by the preparation "recipe" suggested by the late Dr. Griffith-Thomas:

"Think yourself empty.
Read yourself full.
Write yourself clear.
Pray yourself hot."

5

Aiming the Lesson

After the teacher has secured a grasp of the lesson material, his next task is to select a single aim for the lesson. This means that he asks himself the question, "What spiritual result do I want this lesson to accomplish in the lives of the students?" If we may compare the process to a journey, we should say that the gathering together of the baggage would represent the mastering of the lesson material; the choosing of the route and mode of conveyance would correspond to the selecting of the method of teaching; and the determining of the destination and manner of spending our time there would represent the aim of the lesson. A Sunday School lesson is a voyage with a definite purpose, and must be carefully charted. The teacher who starts Nowhere generally gets there.

And it is quite possible for the teacher to get "nowhere" with a lesson. Many of us are acquainted with the type of teaching exemplified in the illustration given by Clarence H. Benson:

Teacher: "Johnnie Jones, you may read the next verse."

Johnnie Jones reads: "And last of all the woman died also. Therefore in the resurrection whose wife shall she be?"

Teacher: "Can any little boy tell me what that means?"

Billie Brown: "Be good."

Teacher: "That is right, Billie; you may read the next verse."

Mr. Benson asks, "How long would a day school last if conducted this way?"

The above method does not represent real teaching; it is rather lightly touching upon as many lessons as there are verses in the lesson text. And the result is that the student leaves with some memories of a dozen or more unrelated facts instead of carrying away imbedded in soul and mind, like a pebble in concrete, one outstanding, gripping lesson.

Someone may ask, "One lesson—is that all we are supposed to give the student during a forty-minute class period?" The fact of the matter is that one main lesson is all that one can effectively impart. Professor James rightly contended that one can make only one point in an hour's lecture. For example, what would happen if an individual attempted to cover New York City in one day? He would see so much that he would not see the city—contradictory as that may sound. It would be far better for him to concentrate upon one object, and plan to spend the day visiting, say, the prominent churches, or noted colleges.

A Sunday School expert has said: "It is better to teach one truth in a dozen ways, or from a dozen angles, than to try to teach a dozen truths in one lesson. That simply cannot be done. A carpenter in making a joint will drive few nails. He will drive them clear through and clinch them at the back. He well knows that too many nails will split the boards and spoil the joint."

Of course this does not mean that the forty minutes are to be consumed in considering one unvarying lesson to the exclusion of interesting details and side-glances. It means that the central aim and lesson shall be like the sun, round which all subordinate thoughts, like planets, revolve. When the Spaniards fought against the Indians of Central and South America, the soldiers were instructed to capture or kill the Cacique, or chief; they knew that to capture the chief was to capture the entire tribe. In like manner the task of the teacher and the class is to capture the "chief" lesson of the text; that must be the teacher's aim. This naturally leads to the question,

How shall I determine the aim of the lesson?

First, by a careful study of the lesson text. For example, if the lesson is found in John 15, the teacher will probably decide: "I must burn into the hearts and minds of my class the imperative need of keeping in close touch with Christ through prayer and the reading of the Word." Or, if the portion is found in Matt. 6:5-15, he may say to himself, "My main task during these forty minutes will be to inspire my pupils with an intense desire to take their Bibles and get alone somewhere with God." Or, let us suppose that the lesson is not of a practical, but of a descriptive nature, and is intended to serve as an introduction to the series for the quarter; for instance, a lesson describing the childhood, education, etc., of Paul the apostle. The teacher will perhaps say to himself, "This is the first lesson of a series on the life of Paul. I must see to it that I leave the students with a clear, vivid idea of the home life and education of a Jewish boy of those days, and then show them that God was preparing Paul for his future work."

Thus we see that the main purpose of the lesson text is to provide a means of directing an outstanding lesson into the hearts and minds of the pupils. "The lesson is a vehicle for carrying the message," writes Marion Lawrance. "The lesson is the bottle; the message is the oil. The lesson is the ship; the message is the cargo. The pupil will leave the lesson behind but will carry the message away. The message alone is what can be transmuted into life. How often we hear Christian men and women say that they do not remember a single fact taught by their Sunday School teachers in earlier years, but they remember the effect of the teaching upon their lives."

Second, the aim of the lesson will be determined by the needs of the pupils. It is the business of the teacher to know the members of his class—their social weaknesses and trials, their enthusiasms, their interests, and their home and school background. By setting this practical knowledge and the lesson material side by side the teacher will be able to decide the aim of his next Sunday's lesson. Mr. Philip Howard, in his book, *A Little Kit of Teacher's Tools* (Sunday School Times Co.), makes some valuable suggestions along this line. "There are several ways by which you can study the members of your class, to find out their interests and their characteristics, and the direct route to the soul and mind of each. See what kind of homes they have; note the type of father and mother, the pictures on the walls, the magazines on the table, the books the family is reading, the order or disorder in the home. Talk with each member of your class, one

at a time, when you are having a walk together, about
the best-liked books, games, work; the pupil's plans
for the year in school, home, or business; plans for
life work; learn who are the pupil's intimate friends.
Make a mental note, or pencil note, of any moral slant
that shows itself in conversation in class or out of
class. You may hear one of your class say that a lie
is sometimes the 'only thing.' You may not be led to
take up the question then, but you have now a glimpse
of the character you are to deal with. Study faces.
Note trivial signs of ill-nature, of suspicion, or friv-
olous or low thinking, and note with equal care the
clear eye, the good color, and the open and frank look."

6

Planning the Lesson

A writer records the following impression of a speech he once heard. "He knew his subject thoroughly, knew far more about it than he could possibly use; but he had not planned his speech. He had not selected his material. He had not arranged it in orderly fashion. Nevertheless, with a courage born of inexperience, he plunged heedlessly, blindly into his speech. He did not know where he was going, but he was on his way. His mind was, in short, a mere hodgepodge, and so was the mental feast he served us. He brought on the ice-cream first, and then placed the soup before us. Fish and nuts came next. And, on top of that, there was something that seemed to be a mixture of soup and ice cream and good red herring."

Certainly no earnest teacher would like to have this said about one of his lessons. Therefore, after familiarizing himself with the lesson material, and determining his aim, he will arrange his material in a logical, orderly way, so that it may effectiv'ly produce the result planned. And this is the subject of the present chapter.

We are now going to watch a teacher at work, and "listen in" as he prepares his next Sunday's lesson, which, let us suppose, is based upon Matthew 6:5-15. He folds two large sheets of paper in pamphlet form so that they will slip easily into his quarterly. Having thought himself empty, and read himself full, he prepares to write himself clear. Of course he is not going to depend entirely upon his notes while teaching; he will merely glance at them occasionally for reference. The main purpose of making an outline is to fix the lesson in the mind in a logical, orderly fashion. It is advisable to write neatly, for a carefully prepared outline is worth keeping, especially if the teacher is also a preacher.

The simplest and most practical way of arranging a lesson outline is the following threefold division:

I. PREPARATION (or, the Start).

II. PRESENTATION (or, the Progress).

III. CONCLUSION (or, the Finish).

The teacher writes on his paper in capitals the title: THE CHRISTIAN AT PRAYER, and underneath, the lesson-text reference. The date and name of the lesson series might be added for reference. And, if he desires to sacrifice a portion of the quarterly, he may cut out the verses for class study, and paste them on his outline.

He will then write in capitals:

I. PREPARATION

A successful teacher has well said, "The beginning and the ending! These are the hardest things in almost any activity to manage adroitly. For example, at a social function aren't the most trying feats the graceful entrance and the graceful leave-taking? In a business interview aren't most difficult tasks the winning approach and the successful close?" The same holds true in teaching a Sunday School lesson. The purpose of the presentation is to make an opening into the minds and hearts of the listeners; the purpose of the conclusion is to clinch the lesson after it has entered. And how does the preparation accomplish its purpose? By capturing the students' attention and interest. "Much depends upon a proper approach," writes Lawrance. "The teacher should not dump out his material upon the class, like pouring apples into a basket. The approach should be catchy as a fishhook, so that it will hold the minute it strikes, but it should also be like a harpoon, that will make it hold when it is in."

In this section of the outline the teacher will have three underlined headings:

1. Get the student to thinking.
2. Arouse his interest.
3. State the subject of the lesson.

Let us enlarge upon each of these points.

1. *Get the student to thinking.* (Refer back to points one and two in Chapter II.) In this part of the lesson the teacher will begin with the student's own ideas, for teaching is explaining new truths with the help of truths already understood by the learner. Dr. Weigle in his masterly book, *The Pupil and the Teacher* (Lutheran Publication Society), writes, "You must not introduce new material here. You may revive his memories of former lessons, or call up things he has read, or remind him of definite experiences that he has had. In any case the one great question is—is this idea one that will help him to understand the lesson as he ought to understand it?"

Let us listen to the teacher's thoughts. "Now, what do they already know about the subject that will 'hook on' to the new material and make them want to know more? Most of them were present last Sunday and heard the missionary describe the prayer wheels of Tibet, by the use of which a native prays as many times as he turns a wheel. I will ask them what they think about that kind of praying. Then I will show them how important it is to know the right way, as taught in our lesson.

"In case the pupils are listless or disorderly, and it looks as if I may have difficulty in securing their attention, I may use the following story: 'During one of his evangelistic meetings D. L. Moody, the famous evangelist, called upon a brother to pray. He began, but it seemed that he did not know where to stop. Five, ten, fifteen minutes passed, and the people became restless. Finally, Moody stood up with hymn book in hand and announced, "We will now sing a hymn while the brother is finishing his prayer." It was a good thing that the evangelist was led to take this step, for in the congregation was a gifted young man who became so wearied with the over-lengthy prayer that he was about to leave. But, as he later said, Moody's common sense impressed him, so that he stayed, and came forward at the altar call. He later became a world-known missionary.'

"I am confident," continues the teacher, "that they will see the point of the story and appreciate the value of knowing the *right* way to pray. However, I shall use this only in an emergency, for it is possible that they may be taken up with the humor of the story rather than with its lesson."

2. *Arouse the learner's interest.* So far we have made a *contact* with the student. And now that we have introduced the subject to him, our next task is to keep him so interested in the topic that his attention is held. How may this be done? The knowledge of an important truth concerning human nature may prove helpful at this point. Every descendant of Adam is fundamentally selfish. Not that everyone yields to that selfishness, but the instinct is there. In whom is the average person most interested? In himself, of course! For example, if you knew that the evening paper contained a paragraph concerning yourself, which portion of the paper would you read first? The answer is obvious. A keen student of human nature has said that the average person would rather listen to you say something nice about him than hear you discuss the ten greatest men in history.

Now this has not been mentioned to poke fun at the fact that we are more or less interested in ourselves, but to show how this knowledge may be used for a good purpose. Even the Lord Jesus appealed to self-interest in order to teach unselfishness when He said, "Thou shalt love thy neighbor *as thyself*"; also in the Golden Rule, "Therefore all things whatsoever ye would that men should do to *you*, do ye even so to them." How may this principle be used to interest a student in a lesson? By showing him the value of the lesson, and how much the knowledge is going to mean to him personally.

Let us listen further to the teacher's musings: "If I am to hold their attention on this subject for perhaps twenty-five or thirty minutes, I simply must create within them a *burning desire to know* the lesson. If I succeed in getting them aroused and excited over the lesson, they will be ready for the truth. Naturally, they will be interested in possessing power. So I will explain that prayer is the greatest force in the universe—that it moves the Hand that moves the world. I may give an illustration showing something that prayer has actually accomplished. I must make them to understand clearly what prayer will mean in their own lives."

3. *State your subject definitely.* The teacher has introduced his subject to the student and secured his interest; he now states definitely the thing to be learned. "The subject should be brief and attractive," writes Dr. Weigle. "It should be worth remembering and should serve as a clue for a subsequent recall of the lesson. Whenever possible, it should contain a proper name, and the lesson event or characterization. 'Abraham's willingness to offer up Isaac,' 'Joseph's kindness to his brothers,' 'Joshua's battle against five kings,' etc."

In the lesson we are using for a model, the subject might be stated as follows: "Jesus teaches right and wrong ways of praying," or, "Jesus teaches us how to pray."

The *aim* of the lesson has already been determined by the teacher (see previous chapter); this he does not state to the class. He tells them what they are going to study, but keeps in his own mind the aim that he purposes to accomplish.

Before leaving this section of the outline two suggestions are necessary: (1) It may seem that much time has been consumed in describing the preparation of the lesson; actually, however, the introduction should occupy only a small fraction of the lesson period. By careful planning the teacher will be able to cover much ground, and yet be brief and to the point. (2) In this part of the lesson the students' activity should be enlisted as much as possible. They should be "drawn out" by skillful questions to express themselves.

Having planned the introduction, the teacher now prepares the main part of the lesson known as the

II. PRESENTATION

In this section the teacher will—

1. Summarize the lesson.
2. Develop the lesson.
3. Illustrate the lesson.

1. Summarize the Lesson

A guide who is about to conduct a party of tourists through an interesting piece of country may perhaps take them first to a high hill, and give them a bird's-eye view of the land, thus enabling them to take in at a glance the beauty of the territory they are to traverse slowly afterward. In a similar manner the teacher will first state the high points of the lesson, so that the student may see it as a whole. Perhaps some have been puzzled as to what to do with that mysterious looking assemblage of facts known as an "outline." Well, here is one purpose: it enables the teacher to present the essential facts of the lesson in an orderly manner.

Therefore the teacher writes out the following outline, which, let us suppose, is the one given in the quarterly, or in some other teacher's guide:

I. WRONG WAYS.   Matt. 6:5,7.

    1. The Jewish error: "showing off."

    2. The Gentile error: senseless repetition.

II. RIGHT WAYS.   Matt. 6:6, 8.

    1. Reality: pray to be seen and heard of God.

    2. Intelligence: commune with an intelligent Being.

III. A PATTERN: THE LORD'S PRAYER. Matt. 6:9-15.

    1. Invocation.

    2. God's—

        name.

        kingdom.

        will.

    3. Man's—

        material needs.

        forgiveness.

        deliverance.

    4. Doxology.

Of course, the teacher should not read off the outline in a stiff, formal manner. The skeleton should be clothed with the flesh of conversation. For example: "Let us consider, first of all, some wrong ways of praying, mentioned by Christ; namely, praying with a wrong motive of performing before people, and praying in a parrot-like, senseless fashion. We shall find that there are two remedies for these errors: first, secret prayer in the presence of God; second, remembering that in addressing God we are speaking to an intelligent Person. Following this we shall study the model of intelligent prayer, commonly known as the

Lord's Prayer, in which is set forth the correct manner of approaching and petitioning God."

2. Develop the Lesson

We have now reached the main part of the lesson, in which the teacher, like a skilled artisan, begins work upon the facts, fitting them together in their proper relationship, clearing up difficult questions, and, in general, organizing the material so that it will produce the result planned.

How shall he go about this rather complicated task? That will depend upon the method he is following. If the teacher has a class in the lower grades, where the basis of the lesson is a story, the details of the story must be thoroughly mastered. If the lecture method is used it will be well to make a detailed outline. But, for the sake of illustration, let us suppose that the teacher has a class in one of the higher grades; it is likely that he will use the question, or discussion, method, which seems to be the most common. If so, the best outline will be a sufficient number of well-prepared, thought-provoking questions, each of which shall constitute a center of discussion of some important topic. Did you ever throw a stone into a river and watch the ever widening circles it produced? This illustrates the effect of each of these "developing" questions; they stimulate the class into developing a topic. Additional questions may have to be added to draw out the full answer.

To illustrate: the teacher begins preparing his list of questions (which we shall indicate by italics).

(1) *Notice verse 5. What is a hypocrite?* This

will provide the starting point for a lesson on hypocrisy. It will stir the minds of the students and bring to the surface any information they possess concerning the subject; for the skillful teacher first makes use of the pupils' own ideas. After the class had had a moment to think over the question, and some answers have been given, the teacher may "draw out" the class (remember the definition of "educate") with questions like the following: *"Would you apply the term 'hypocrite' to a Christian, who, through weakness falls into sin? Would it apply to a church member who has never been really converted? Or to a person who was once soundly converted but is now living in sin? Now look at verse 5, and give Jesus' own description of what constitutes a hypocrite."*

The class is now ready for another question.

(2) *Do you believe that the Lord was forbidding public prayer? See verse 6.* This question is the "starter" of a new topic; it has stirred the students' ideas, bringing them to the surface of their minds. Those ideas may now be drawn out and developed by questions like the following: *"Can you give a definite proof that Jesus believed in public prayer?"* (as we shall see later, *yes* and *no* answers are not sufficient; they give no evidence that the pupil has been really thinking). *"If by being 'seen of men' the Lord was not forbidding public prayer, what was He forbidding?"* etc.

This will suffice to illustrate the nature and use of an interrogative outline. As we leave this topic, however, may we suggest the following "forget-me-not's":

(1) Remember the time-limit and select those questions that touch the high points of the lesson.

(2) Remember your aim, and make the answers contribute to the accomplishing of your purpose. If we compare the lesson activities to a wheel, the hub would represent the aim, the spokes would correspond to the topics of the lesson, and the rim, to the lives of the students.

3. Illustrate the Lesson

For the sake of review let us return to the illustration of the building of a house:

(1) The mastering of the material and the selecting of the aim corresponds, let us say, to the making of the blueprints and specifications, or the decision as to the material to be used and the plan to be followed.

(2) The preparation of the lesson represents the laying of the foundation.

(3) In summarizing the lesson we erect the framework.

(4) The questions call for the worked-over sections that the student has been requested to make from the raw material of the assignment.

(5) By means of recitation and discussion the teacher fills in the framework.

Now, by the use of illustration, the windows and light-fixtures are put into the building. Illustrations illuminate the subject, help the student to understand, and thus hold his interest. Therefore, at this point it is well for the teacher to prepare a written list of illustrations; or, if he plans to make use of the blackboard or some objects, he will make note of the fact. The value of illustrations can **hardly** be overestimated in the exposition of a lesson. **So** important is the topic that we shall later devote **an entire** chapter to its consideration.

We are now ready for the finishing **touches on** the building, so we come to the

III. CONCLUSION

To vary the illustration: in the Preparation we set the nails; in the Presentation we hammer them down; in the Conclusion we clinch them. Since the purpose of the conclusion is to make certain that the lesson is deeply imbedded in mind and heart, the teacher will make a twofold appeal:

To the mind. The high points of the lesson must be summed up in order to be sure that the student takes these home with him; that is, mentally. In order to find out whether or not the pupils have retained the truths imparted, the teacher permits them to do the talking. He may say to them, "We have time for a brief review before the bell rings. Will someone please give us the title of the lesson that we decided upon at the beginning of our lesson? What was the first wrong way of praying that Christ denounced? And what remedy did He prescribe? Now, what was the second wrong method He exposed? And the remedy He prescribed? Name the pattern prayer which He taught to His disciples. Someone please mention the God-ward petitions. And the manward petitions."

To the heart. At the beginning the teacher set himself to create within the student's mind a burning desire to *know*. He now comes to an even more important task; namely, to create within the student a burning desire to *act* upon that knowledge.

A distinguished scientist once said, "The great end of life is not knowledge, but action." Knowledge must be translated into action. What was said concerning a class of boys is worthy of general application: "Too often in our teaching we are obliged to stop at theory. This savors of unreality. Theory and advice are not what the boy wants. A result such as this fails to connect with actual powers and responsibilities of life. No boy wants mere advice. No boy wants pure theory. What he wants is the real thing. What he is interested in is genuine activity."

Let us apply this truth to the lesson we have been using as a model. The teacher may say to the class: "The best way to learn how to swim is—to swim; the best way to learn to skate is—to skate. We learn by doing. Now, the best way to learn how to pray is to get busy and pray. I am confident that the lesson we have studied will become a lasting blessing to us as we determine to set apart some time daily for prayer, meditation, and Bible reading."

It is impossible to set down hard and fast rules in regard to the method of applying the lesson; all depends upon the circumstances, and the leading of God's Spirit. There are times when, if the teacher has taught well, no formal application will be necessary; the Word will do its own work. Sometimes an indirect suggestion may be more effective than direct exhortation. Notice how the Lord applied the Parable of the Good Samaritan (Luke 10:25-37). After telling the story, the Lord might have made a direct application, saying to the lawyer: "The very fact that you ask such a question as, 'Who is my neighbor?' indicates that you lack the neighborly spirit; for, if you *were* a real neighbor you should know instinctively that *anyone* who needs your help is your neighbor. Manifest the same spirit as that Samaritan, and you will have a perfect answer to your question." But the Lord used the indirect application. He made the questioner express himself, by asking the question, "Which of these three, thinkest thou, was neighbor unto him that fell among the thieves?" He answered, "He that shewed mercy on him." Having drawn out the lawyer, He clinched the lesson with the command, "Go thou and do likewise." There is a rebuke in these words, but it is indirect, and the lawyer is left with something to think upon for many a day.

Notice that the Lord caused the lawyer practically to make his own application. In a similar manner the teacher may induce the students to express themselves, as is suggested by the following: "We have now the knowledge as to the right way of praying. But is it sufficient to know *how* to pray? Will knowledge *about* prayer bring about a revival? Then how must knowing be completed? And the lesson might well close with the answer, "By doing."

SUMMARY

The time limit should be kept in mind in preparing and arranging the lesson material. The lesson may be compared to a boat trip, at the end of which we are expecting the teacher to throw out the gang-plank and unload the passengers on schedule time. Practice and experience will enable the teacher to know what portions of the lesson to emphasize, and what portions to eliminate in order to make the lesson fit the lesson period.

The teacher's written outline should be brief—a mere skeleton of the lesson, with which to refresh his memory.

It should be remembered that the lesson plan explained in this chapter is not intended to cramp the teacher's liberty by forcing his lesson into a cast-iron formula; rather it is designed as a guide to the orderly arrangement and presentation of his material. "Even if you have prepared the best possible outline," writes Mr. Suter, "you may still encounter a situation in the classroom which will throw you off the track. This is sure to happen sometimes. Don't let it discourage you. There is such a thing as a legitimate reason for being thrown off the track. Perhaps a pupil will bring up some genuinely important question which presses for an answer at the moment. It may be your golden opportunity. Remember that the ultimate purpose of teaching religion is to influence lives." It may be necessary and wise to be thrown off the track for a portion of the time, but "it is important to have a track from which to be thrown off."

We have covered quite a stretch of ground in this chapter. Let us look back and get a bird's-eye view of the plan of the lesson:

I. PREPARATION.

Purpose: to prepare the mind and heart of the pupil, by—

1. Getting him to think;
2. Arousing his interest;
3. Stating the subject.

II. PRESENTATION.

Purpose: to impart the main facts of the lesson, by—

1. Summarizing the lesson;
2. Developing the lesson by question, discussion, and explanation;
3. Illustrations.

III. CONCLUSION.

Purpose: to sum up the lesson and apply it to life by a twofold appeal:

1. An appeal to the mind;
2. An appeal to the heart.

7

Keeping the Class Awake

In this chapter we are to consider the importance and means of securing and holding the attention and interest of the class.

The teacher's problem and its solution may be briefly and simply stated as follows:

1. What is his task? To implant the lesson within the minds and hearts of the pupils.

2. How shall he accomplish this? First of all, by securing their attention.

3. How may he secure their attention? By getting them interested.

4. How shall he gain their interest? By comparing the lesson to things they understand, and in which they are interested; in other words, by using their idea.

To reverse the order: if he appeals to their ideas, he will win their interest; if he gains their interest, he will hold their attention; and if he succeeds in holding their attention, he will be able effectively to impart the lesson.

ATTENTION

What is attention? It has been defined as "the steady application of the mind to any object or truth." An attentive pupil is one who is concentrating and focusing the powers of his mind upon what the teacher is saying or doing in connection with the lesson. We say *lesson* because it is possible for a pupil to be gazing steadfastly at the teacher, in an attitude of apparent interest, while his mind may be a thousand miles away. It has been said, "A pupil may look without seeing, listen without being conscious of hearing, and hear without comprehending. He may sit and dream. The mind has inner as well as outer gates. The outer gates admit merely to the courtyard of the mind. A great many pupils keep the inner doors closed to much of the teaching done by teachers." During a gospel meeting in an African village, there was one woman who scarcely moved her eyes from the missionary's face. She seemed to be listening with rapt attention. "There is one woman who is being gripped by the message," thought the missionary. After the service she approached this woman to follow up this display of attention; but, to her disappointment, the heathen woman said, "I have been looking at that gold tooth of yours; please tell me where you got it." She had displayed interest—but not in the subject.

There are two kinds of attention: voluntary and spontaneous. In voluntary attention the listener compels himself by an act of the will to pay attention to the subject. It is not a lasting attitude, for the listener will either glide into spontaneous interest or will lose interest altogether. The latter is more likely to occur than the former.

Attention is spontaneous when it is attracted to an object or subject without effort or strain. All other matters are for the time banished, and the pupil's interest is held without conscious effort on his part. Spontaneous attention is the best, and it is inspired by interest. If the teacher fails to make his lesson interesting, the pupil will probably allow his mind to wander from the subject. One reason for this is that the mind cannot concentrate long upon an unchanging object. Variety and change are essential to interest. The teacher must therefore vary the lesson by turning it round and round, so to speak, and exhibiting it from many angles. He will use the telescope, figuratively speaking, to give a bird's-eye view of the lesson; or, he may use the microscope to show the hidden beauty of a section of a text; coming to a dark corner of the story, he will turn on the flashlight of illustration; or perhaps he will use the brush and canvas to paint a word picture of some Biblical scene. All these activities, and others of a similar nature, are involved in making a lesson interesting.

It is imperatively necessary that the teacher secure and hold the attention of the class, for attention is the only channel through which he can convey his ideas to the listeners. To say that the class is not paying attention is to say that the class is learning nothing, and that the teacher is talking into empty air.

Moreover, it is positively harmful to teach without attention. "Every time you permit disorder, trifling, or wandering, you are helping to lower and vitiate the mental character of your pupils," writes Professor Fitch. "You are encouraging them to a bad habit. You are in fact doing something to prevent them from ever becoming thoughtful readers, diligent observers, and earnest listeners as long as they live."

INTEREST

The securing of interest is of the utmost importance in education; one educator asserts that it is not a means but the end of education. The pupil may forget a multitude of facts that he has been taught, but if the teacher has so taught as to make the student feel that the Bible is the most wonderful book in the world, and the Christian life the highest activity for man, he has succeeded. Let us suppose that a six-months' course in Old Testament history is given in a teacher-training class. We may be sure of two things: first, all the facts of the Old Testament cannot be mastered in that short period; second, the students will forget many of the details. But if the conclusion of the course finds the students gripped with the Divine plan, power, and beauty of the Word; if it finds them conscious of their lack of knowledge and hungry for more, then the course has accomplished its highest end.

The average pupil is simply full of ideas, desires, and impulses that may be classed as interests. These may be enlisted on the side of evil, worldliness, and secondary things; on the other hand, they may be enlisted for God and spiritual things. The task of the Sunday School teacher is to draw out those interests and bind them up with the highest values of life. Take for instance the following case: five days a week the student attends classes in history, geography, science, and other subjects under instructors who put life and interest into their instruction. He goes to church on Sunday and listens to a dry, lifeless, and formal presentation of the gospel. What is the result? He will be likely to conclude that history, science, and other subjects are of the greatest importance, and that religion is a rather dull and meaningless affair.

From what has been said it is apparent that the teacher must do more than interest the students; he must interest them in the *right thing*. He must do more than make the lesson period interesting—he must interest the class in the *lesson*. If the teacher tells a humorous story that has no connection with the lesson, they will remember the story but forget the lesson. However, in cases of emergency, the teacher may find it necessary to depart from this rule. Dr. Weigle writes, "The teacher beginning work with an unruly gang of boys or with a self-satisfied, giggling bevy of girls must win them first in any way he can." He or she must first make the contact between the pupils and himself, before making it between them and the lesson. However, this procedure should be like "the hammer and saw and axe in a Pullman coach, emergency tools, only for use in the case of a smash-up, a total wreck, and threatening death and disaster."

USING THE STUDENT'S VIEWPOINT

When does a subject or activity become interesting? When it gives a person an opportunity to express the ideas and powers that are within him. Therefore the teaching that interests is that which appeals to the pupil's own ideas (refer to Chapter II). The purpose is to—

1. Make him understand the truth.
2. Make him welcome the truth.

1. *Make the pupils understand the truth by presenting the lesson in terms and ideas drawn from their own experience.* "Boy's-eye Views of the Sunday School," the title of a book published by the Sunday

School Times, aptly suggests the truth we are considering; namely, that to interest the pupil we must get his viewpoint and see the truth through his eyes. What Sir John Adams said concerning the preacher applies also to the teacher: "Show me a successful preacher and I will show you a man who is able, metaphorically, to stand in the pulpit and sit in the pew at one and the same time. He must look through his hearers' eyes and present his ideas against *their* backgrounds." In like manner the teacher must see the truth through the eyes of his students. In the book just mentioned is a picture of a boys' class. There sits the teacher, a rather austere-looking man, with his eyes upon his quarterly. He may be interested in the lesson himself, but it is evident that the students are not. One of the boys is glancing longingly at the clock; two are engaged in a vivacious conversation of their own; while a third, with a look of boredom on his face, is saying, "They're awful green about what boys like." This will not happen to the teacher who plans his lessons with the following question in mind: "What idea is already in the mind of the scholar which will enable him to grasp the meaning of the idea that I wish to explain to him today?" Let us study some examples of this principle.

The Divine Teacher Himself explained truth from His listeners' viewpoint. He came with a message that involved the deepest truths concerning God, man, and human existence. How did He make these truths clear to the simple, unlettered Galileans? By telling them that the kingdom of God was *like* some things they already understood:

The Kingdom of Heaven is *like* a mustard seed.

The Kingdom of Heaven is *like* the king's marriage feast.

The Kingdom of Heaven is *like* a man who sowed good seed.

The Kingdom of Heaven is *like* a net let down, etc.

Study the way in which He called Andrew, Peter, James and John into active service. Matt. 4:18-20. He might have said: "Leave your occupation and become My disciples, and I will train you in the work of persuading men to forsake selfishness and sin, and to live lives of righteousness in the service of God." That would have expressed His meaning; but the Lord Jesus had a more pointed and arousing mode of appeal. Knowing that these men were fishermen, engaged in their occupation, He said, "Follow Me and I will make you fishers of men." What better way could be imagined for calling fishermen to missionary work! The Lord knew the "point of contact" in these men, and connected a work that was new to them with an occupation in which they had been engaged most of their lives. "Fishers of *men!*" Peter must have reasoned quickly. "I know what He means. We have been transferring fish from *life unto death;* now we are to draw men from the sea of wickedness, so often described by our rabbis (Isa. 57:20), and lead them from *death unto life.*" That the Lord's appeal touched their minds and hearts is indicated by the fact that "they straightway left their nets, and followed Him."

The following list of questions (quoted by Dr. Schmauk, a Lutheran educator) shows how a difficult subject may be made clear to a class of children. The teacher is describing David's prayer of penitence as recorded in the fifty-first Psalm.

"David is bad because he has done many sins, and has an unclean heart, and yet he is good because he is praying to God. Can a man be both good and bad?" (An uncompromising "No.")

"Well, let's see. When a blacksmith comes home from work is he clean or dirty?" "Dirty."

"But after he has washed himself and sits down to eat his supper and read his newspaper, is he still dirty?" "No, sir."

"Is he clean now?" "Yes, sir."

"So the man can be both clean and dirty?" "Yes, sir."

"At the same time?" "No, sir."

"But he can be dirty at one time and clean at another?" "Yes, sir."

"Now what makes the dirty man into a clean man?" "Washing."

"And what did David want God to do with his heart?" "Wash it." "Make it clean."

"Are we told in the Psalm that God washed it?" (Opposing answers—"Yes," and "No.")

"Well, can God do anything He wishes to do?" "Yes, sir."

"Do you think that He wishes men to have unclean hearts?" "No, sir."

"Then will He wish to clean David's heart?" "Yes, sir."

"And He can do anything He wishes?" "Yes, sir."

"Then as soon as David wants God to wash his heart God will do it at once, won't He?" "Yes, sir."

"How long do you think it will take God to wash David's heart?" ("At once." "Quickly." "Immeliately.")

"How long will the blacksmith take to wash himself?" ("Five minutes," "ten minutes," ventured.)

"Will God need as long as that?" "No, sir."

"God does not need any time at all, does He?" "No, sir."

"Then just as David prayed, he was cleansed, and so was at once a good man?" "Yes, sir."

"What makes people ask God to wash them?" (No answer).

"Well, what makes the blacksmith wash himself?" "Because he feels dirty." "Because he would dirty his meat."

"If the blacksmith liked to be dirty, would he go and wash himself?" "No, sir."

"Would the water come and wash him?" "No, sir."

"Then he washes himself because he likes to be clean?" "Yes, sir."

"And he washes himself because he does not like to be dirty?" "Yes, sir."

"And if he wants to be washed, he can be washed at once?" "Yes, sir."

"Then if a man's heart is unclean, it is because he likes it to be unclean?" "Yes, sir."

"And if he wants a clean heart he can get it at once?" "Yes, sir."

Notice how the questioner made clear to the children the difficult subject of spiritual cleansing by comparing it with physical washing, with which they were all (we trust) familiar.

2. *Make the scholars welcome the truth by adapting it to their felt needs.* Let us imagine the case of a class of boys who are to be taught a lesson based on the first chapter of Daniel. The teacher must first get them interested in the lesson. How shall he begin? Certainly not by a theological discourse on the sanctification of the body; theology is above their heads. However, knowing that boys are interested in athletics, he may start out somewhat as follows: "The lesson we are to study this morning is going to be worth more than gold to everyone of you, as far as practical value is concerned. For in this lesson God tells us how we may keep our bodies strong and healthy, and our minds clear and vigorous, so that we may win in the battle and game of life. Daniel found that out by experience when he made up his mind that he was going to do what God had commanded concerning his physical life. Daniel who? I mean that Daniel described in our lesson. Here's the story. . . . "

What we have said concerning teaching the lesson from the viewpoint of the student will explain the imperative necessity of becoming acquainted with the pupils if one is to be a successful teacher. Miss Cather writes, "The mind and heart of the learner is the field in which the sower plants the seed, and the husbandman who knows not the quality of the soil of his farm plot reaps a scanty harvest."

8

Keeping the Teacher Awake

This is really a continuation of our last chapter, "Keeping the Class Awake." Our title for this chapter is chosen with the purpose of suggesting that the attitude of the teacher will largely determine the attitude of the class. He will find himself greatly aided in the securing of attention if he maintains the following attitudes of:

1. Enthusiastic interest.
2. Thorough preparation.
3. Constant vigilance.
4. Christlike charity.

ENTHUSIASTIC INTEREST

A preacher once asked Henry Ward Beecher, "What is the best way of keeping a congregation awake on a hot Sunday afternoon?" His reply was, "Get a long, sharp stick and prod—*the preacher!*" There is great wisdom in that reply. "Every time we speak we determine the attitude of our hearers," Dr. Dale Carnegie tells us. "We hold them in the hollow of our hands. If we are lackadaisical, they will be lackadaisical. If we are reserved they will be reserved. If we are only mildly concerned, they will be only mildly concerned. But if we are deadly in earnest about what we say, and if we say it with feeling and spontaneity and force and contagious conviction, they cannot help from catching our spirit to a degree." The late F. B. Meyer had this truth in mind when he said, "When I find that the people are losing interest I ram myself into the gun and fire myself at the congregation."

All this means that the successful teacher will be eloquent, not with the eloquence of a smooth flow of words, but with the eloquence of a sincere outflowing of truth from the heart. What has been said concerning a sermon certainly applies to a Sunday School lesson: "You will find that the sermons you enjoy preaching the most and the ones which actually accomplish the most good in the lives of your people will be those sermons which you take largely out of your own interiors. They are bone of your bone, flesh of your flesh, the children of your own mental labor, the output of your own creative energy. The sermons which live and move, and enter into the temple, walking, and leaping and praising God, the sermons which enter into the hearts of men causing them to mount with wings like eagles and to walk in the ways of duty and not faint—these real sermons are the ones which are actually born from the vital energies of the man who utters them."

And there is a sure way whereby the teacher may secure this heart preparation. It is the way of prayer. Let him take his lesson outline into the presence of God, and pray over every point and detail, asking God questions about it, pleading for the help of His Spirit, praying that every topic may be burned into his own soul, speaking to Him about the lesson as one would discuss it with a friend. Surely then the teacher will understand what the Psalmist meant when he said,

"My heart was hot within me; while I was musing the fire burned: then spake I with my tongue." Psa. 39:3.

To sum up: if the teacher grips the lesson, and then lets the lesson grip him, he will have no difficulty in making it grip his hearers.

THOROUGH PREPARATION

Dwight L. Moody once set himself to an intensive study of the topic of *Grace*. He became so wrought up with his subject that he seized his hat, hurried into the street, and confronted the first passer-by with the question, "Do you know what grace is?" It is no wonder that thousands were moved by the preaching of this man of God. A teacher may be tempted to depend upon his general knowledge, or to rely upon the fact that he has taught the same lesson before; but if he is wise he will not yield to that temptation. Even though he has studied the identical lesson a few months ago he will not be prepared to face the class unless he sees to it that the lesson is "born again" through the labor of study and prayer.

And the teacher should gather more material than he can possibly use in the lesson. Although it is difficult to explain the fact, yet it is true that the reserve material gives a peculiar force to every word spoken, and inspires the speaker himself with confidence. The necessity for this "super-preparation" is threefold:

For the sake of the lesson. It is related that Miss Ida M. Tarbell, the well known historian, was asked to write a magazine article about the Atlantic Cable. She interviewed the European manager of the principal cable; she studied all manner of cables on display at the British museum; she read books on the history of the cable, and even visited a factory where cables were made. Why did she collect ten times more material than she could use? She knew that the surplus material would give force to every word she wrote just as the water in the great tank supplies the pressure behind the stream of water that issues from the faucet. The average teacher cannot, of course, put a similar amount of work on each lesson, but he will understand the principle.

For the teacher's own sake. If we had invited a company of people to a meal, and were uncertain as to whether there was sufficient food to go around, would we feel very comfortable, especially if we knew they were all hearty eaters? Hardly. Only in the knowledge that we had more than enough could we feel perfectly at ease. The best way for a teacher to feel confident before a class with large appetites for truth is to come before them with an abundant supply of well-cooked spiritual food.

For the sake of the class. In the words of Professor Palmer: "In preparing a lecture I find that I always have to work hardest on the things I do not say. The things I am sure to say I can easily get up. They are obvious and easily accessible. But they, I find, are not enough. I must have a broad background of knowledge which does not appear in speech. I have to go over my entire subject and see how the things I am to say look in their various relations, tracing out connections which I shall not present to my class. One might ask, What is the use of this? Why prepare more matter than can be used? Every successful teacher knows. I cannot teach up to the edge of my knowledge without a fear of falling off. My pupils discover this fear and my words are ineffective. They feel the influence of what I do not say. One cannot precisely explain it; but when I move freely across my subject as if it mattered little on what part I rest, they get a sense of assured power which is compulsive and fructifying."

Thorough preparation pays; for the teacher will discover that he is obtaining a grasp of God's Word that he could not receive by mere reading or listening. He will understand by experience why many teachers have declared that "the best way to learn is to teach."

CONSTANT VIGILANCE

A well known evangelist was addressing an audience in a large tent. He began his sermon along the lines of exhortation to the defense of the faith. Suddenly he changed the tenor of his message and related a heart-touching narrative that left the audience in tears. Why did he change his topic? With the eye of an experienced public speaker, he noticed that he was losing the attention of the audience because the particular sermon with which he began was not gripping them. Realizing the uselessness of preaching without attention, he deliberately changed his subject in order to regain their interest. And he was able to make this change because he was watching his audience closely. In a similar manner the teacher should carefully observe the attitude of the pupils. If he discerns a waning interest, exhibited in dreamy eyes and bored countenances, he should at once do something to recover their attention; for example, he might step to the blackboard and begin to write, or he might tell a story, give an illustration, or ask some thought-provoking question.

CHRIST-LIKE CHARITY

Some truths are so true, so much taken for granted, and so fully believed, that they frequently lie down, so to speak, in our minds and go fast asleep. The duty of love is one of them. But it should be constantly stirred into action, for of all forces that bind the teacher to the pupil, and therefore to his teaching, love is the greatest. And they will recognize and respond to kindly sympathy and interest, for, as has been said, "The well known human race is quick to detect whether a talk is coming from above the eyebrows or back of the breastbone." And without the affection that binds heart to heart our teaching will be as sounding brass and a tinkling cymbal. As we pray for each member of the class by name, asking God to give us wisdom to help each one, according to his individual need, we shall bind ourselves to the pupils with the golden chains of Christian sympath and devotion.

In this and the previous chapter we have discusse principles and rules for stimulating interest. In ou. next three chapters we shall consider practical method for putting those principles and rules into practice. They are as follows:

1. The use of illustrations.
2. The use of blackboard and objects
3. Story-telling.

9

Making Your Meaning Clear

The importance of illustrations in illuminating the lesson can hardly be over-emphasized. What windows and lights are to a house so illustrations are to a lesson. "One picture is worth ten thousand words," say the Chinese. The teacher who would succeed will therefore turn his pupils' ears into eyes and make them see what he is telling them. For example, compare the following statements:

(1) "If we fall into sin it is foolish to remain in that condition. Let us go immediately to God and obtain forgiveness."

(2) "What would you think of a person who, after losing his footing and tumbling into a muddy ditch, should stretch out and lie down, bemoaning his accident and miry condition? We should think him foolish indeed. A wise man would scramble out as soon as possible, brush the mud from his clothes, go home, take a bath, and change garments. One striking difference between a sheep and a hog is that if a sheep falls into the mud it will bleat, while the hog will simply lie there and wallow. Christ's sheep will not, and should not, stay in the mire of sin if they happen to fall there through temptation and weakness."

In the first statement the students simply *hear* the truth; in the second, they *see* it. And they will remember the second statement more easily, for pic-

tures embed themselves in the mind like bullets in a
tree. It is well, therefore, to cultivate the art of speaking in pictures. For example, one writer who wished
to express the thought that it is useless to attempt
to improve upon that which is perfect, said it in a
series of pictures: "To gild refined gold, to paint the
lily, to throw perfume on the violet." He made us
see what he was saying.

Further emphasis is placed upon the importance
of illustrations by the place they occupy in the teaching of Christ, who was constantly telling the people
what the Kingdom of heaven was *like* by the use of
parables. "Mourning and weeping, laughing and danc-
ing, wealth and poverty, hunger and thirst, health and
sickness, children's play and politics, gathering and
scattering, the leaving of home, life in the inn, marriage and funeral, the splendid house of the living and
the grave of the dead, the sower and the reaper in
the field, the lord of the vintage among his vines, the
idle workman in the market-place, the shepherd
searching for the sheep, the dealer in pearls of the
sea, and then again, the woman at the home, anxious
over the barrel of meal or leaven, or the lost piece of
money, the surly official, the earthly food that perishes
—all these pictures enliven His discourse and make
it clear even to those who are children in mind."

Let us consider some principles governing the
right use of illustrations.

1. *The illustration should be clearer than the truth
it is meant to illustrate.* An explanation which requires an explanation is really no explanation. The
same is true of an illustration. The purpose of illustration is to illuminate a subject that may be obscure

to the listeners; but if the illustration is not clear to them the darkness is doubled. A preacher once addressed a group of children as follows: "Now I will explain hope, so all these girls can go home and tell their mothers what hope is. Now, children, you know that this beautiful stream of water that runs behind this meeting house is composed of two elements, oxygen and hydrogen; so hope is composed of desire and expectation." Instead of casting light on the subject this speaker simply plunged the children into thick darkness, for how many of them understood the meaning of the words, "element," "hydrogen," "oxygen," or "expectation"?

2. *The illustration should appeal to something within the pupil's own experience.* The fact that an illustration appeals to the teacher does not necessarily guarantee its appeal to the student. We are told of an address that once was made to a group of children on the text, "The little foxes spoil the vines." The speaker's purpose was to describe the damage wrought to character by small vices or weaknesses. At first sight the illustration seems vivid and apt. But let us examine it more closely. How many of the children had ever seen a fox or known much about one? How many had ever seen a vine? In fact, they were not living in a country where the destruction of vines by foxes was an actual fact or a topic of conversation. Thus the illustration failed to make the point of contact with the pupils.

The sermon would have been driven home more successfully if the speaker had brought with him a specked apple and a knife and explained to the children that a small decayed spot will spread over the entire apple (illustrated by a rotten apple) unless it is cut out. Such an illustration would have been within the reach of their experience, for probably every one of them had munched apples and tasted the bitter of the spoiled part.

Let us look at another example. Some missionaries were translating the Bible into the dialect of an African tribe. They came to the verse: "Though your sins be as scarlet, they shall be as white as snow." To translate this verse literally would have been to make it meaningless to the natives, who had never seen snow. In fact, they had no word for snow. But they had eaten many a cocoanut, and knew by experience the whiteness of the meat. So the missionaries translated the verse as follows: "Though your sins be as scarlet they shall be as white as the meat of a cocoanut." This rendering may sound somewhat strange to us, but it brought the truth within the range of the experience of the natives.

3. *Illustrations should have a real connection with the lesson.* They should not be dragged in and forcibly attached to the lesson merely to ornament it. Illustrations are not ends in themselves, but simply helps to the understanding of the lesson. Like eyeglasses, they should be looked through and not looked at. The teacher should ask himself the questions, "Is it needed?" "Will it fit?" "Is it appropriate?" Like a flashlight it should not be carried for an ornament, but as a means of illumination.

4. *Avoid the use of too many illustrations.* While a house that has no windows is a dark place, a house that is all windows is a poor house. When several

illustrations are used to explain one point the effect may be confusing to the student.

5. *Avoid illustrations that leave a bad impression.* We refer to those illustrations which, by their coarseness, or grotesqueness either disgust or amuse the class, so that the truth is really obscured rather than clarified. For example, the drawing power of an atmosphere charged with the presence of the Holy Spirit has often been compared to being exposed to measles. This illustration is inappropriate for two reasons: first, the nature and power of God's Spirit is not explained by comparing that influence to a *disease;* second, such an illustration, because of its coarseness is not likely to inspire reverence. Rather, it may provoke chuckles, instead of devotion.

Looking at the subject from another aspect, Marion Lawrance writes: "The writer has wholly abandoned all stories and illustrations in his public addresses that would tend to send anyone away feeling badly. This means that no stories about stuttering people, or referring to deformities, such as hunchbacks, harelips, clubfeet, etc., will ever be told. It is not kind or Christian to send some unfortunate person away from the meeting feeling that you might have made your point without reminding him of his infirmity."

6. *Avoid illustrations that may suggest a wrong idea.* The following example of this principle is quoted by Dr. Weigle. "A Sunday School was listening to a talk upon the fixedness of habits formed in youth, and to make it clear the speaker said, 'Boys, do they ever lay cement walks in this neighborhood?' Every eye was riveted upon him as they answered, 'Yes!'

'Did you know,' he continued, 'that if you were to take a sharp-pointed stick and write your name in the cement while it was soft, it would harden and remain there as long as the walk lasted? Of course,' he hastily added, as a significant expression appeared on their faces, 'no boy here would be mean enough to do such a thing.' But it was too late—the picture had done its work, and the purpose of handing down autographs to posterity would be executed at the first opportunity."

HOW SHALL I APPLY ILLUSTRATIONS?

There are two ways:

1. STATE YOUR ILLUSTRATION AND APPLY THE TRUTH. For example:

The Illustration. It is said that when a runner feels that his breath is about gone, his lungs are bursting, and he is so completely exhausted that he can hold out no longer, something remarkable happens. He feels a sudden inrush of strength, fatigue disappears, and he continues his course as fresh as when he first began. This inrush of new strength is known as the "second wind."

The Application. This illustration will help us to understand what the prophet meant when he declared, "They that wait upon the Lord shall renew their strength." If, while running our spiritual race, we reach the place where our strength is almost gone and we feel like "quitting," let us trust God and hold on. For, if we wait upon the Lord, we shall receive our "second wind," spiritually speaking.

2. STATE YOUR TRUTH AND APPLY THE ILLUSTRATION.

The Statement. Many people agree that prayer operates in the spiritual realm, inspiring our souls, strengthening our wills, and bringing us into contact with God. But some fail to realize that prayer operates also in the realm of material affairs, changing conditions, and bringing things to pass.

The Illustration. Many years ago George Mueller founded an orphanage in England where over ten thousand orphans were cared for. Millions of dollars were sent in for the expense of the institution; and yet, surprising to relate, there was no public solicitation of funds. What is the explanation? Only one—the believing prayer of George Mueller.

It is a good plan to state the illustration in such a way as to keep the listener in suspense and pique his curiosity. He will thus be in an alert condition to receive the truth. Supposing the teacher should say, "I was going down Christian street in Jerusalem one day when I met a man clad in the gorgeous robes of an Oriental potentate; and at his side hung the curved gold sword worn only by the descendant of the prophet Mohammed. But this man had none of the appearances of an Arab. He had blue eyes; and the Arab's eyes are always black or brown. . . ." Does this arouse curiosity? Does it make you want to know more? And don't you think that the students who were losing interest would instantly prick up their ears? It has been well said that "An illustration should be opened before the class or before the school just as a Christmas package is opened in the home. The tighter the string, the tighter the expectancy, and particularly if you can't tell from the shape of the box what is in it."

WHERE SHALL I OBTAIN ILLUSTRATIONS?

The best illustrations are those taken from the teacher's own experience and observation. For example, what class would go to sleep if they heard the teacher say, "Now this verse brings to my mind a hair-raising experience I had in the California desert. . . ." Or, "While on my way to work yesterday morning I saw the strangest sight I have witnessed in many a day. . . ." What we have experienced or witnessed can be told with a peculiar force and authority that will compel interest.

The Sunday School quarterly will furnish many illustrations, but it is well to have a reserve supply of illustrations, for nothing helps to regain lost attention like a good story. There are many books of illustrations, which may prove helpful. While it is true that some fail to derive much help from such books, yet, if properly studied, they may be of great value.

Perhaps some have wondered just how to use a notebook in lesson preparation. At the beginning of a new quarter it is an excellent plan to take a little time and "line up" the entire series, getting an idea of the lessons to be covered during the quarter. Having done so, the teacher is now prepared to be on the look-out for suitable illustrations. He may perhaps be walking down the street, when he notices something that would splendidly illustrate Lesson 5. He takes out his notebook (an inexpensive loose-leaf binder is best) and on one page writes the heading, *Lesson 5;* on this page he makes a note of the illustration he wishes to make use of. Again, he may be reading the newspaper and be impressed with an incident that will provide a good "start" for the sixth lesson; once more he takes his notebook, writes on another page the heading, *Lesson 6,* clips the incident from the newspaper and pins it to the page. Or, as he travels to work on the street car he may recall some personal experience that will surely drive home Lesson 11; this he will jot down on a scrap of paper and record permanently when he gets home. And all this is by way of saying that the alert teacher will be on the look-out for lesson material as the wide-awake editor is on the watch for good "copy." And once the "filing" habit is formed it becomes a means of real enrichment to one's teaching.

10

Using the Eye Gate

We are told that eighty-five per cent of our knowledge comes to us by way of the eye. "One seeing is worth a hundred times telling," says a Japanese proverb. And there is no doubt that one of the most impressive and effective ways of teaching is to convey the truth to mind and heart by way of the eye-gate. In all lands objects and pictures provide a simple language for old and young that captures attention, fixes interest, and makes things clear. This being true, it is evident that the eye-gate method of teaching will prove to be an important means of imparting spiritual truth, especially to children. Among the many modes of conveying Bible truths to the heart through the eye-gate, there are two that we shall consider:

1. Blackboard drawing.
2. The use of objects.

BLACKBOARD DRAWING

The following experience may sound familiar to many a teacher: "I had to contend week after week with a roomful of children who did not even pretend to be interested in what I sought to teach them. They were frankly bored, and seemed able to keep awake only by dint of incessant fidgeting, giggling, or passing of notes. For a whole year the torment continued, and Sundays became to me days of unspeakable dread. No matter what tricks I tried, what games I played, somehow I could not arouse in children any sustained interest in the Bible tales. And then, almost by accident, I hit on the idea of drawing crude maps on the blackboard. They were exceedingly crude, especially in the beginning. I used to scrawl them hurriedly while I talked to the class, cluttering them up with little hills and trees and arrows as the lesson progressed. But their grotesque inaccuracy seemed to make them only the more interesting to the children." Another teacher who complained, "Somehow I seem unable to get the attention of those boys," was advised by the superintendent to try the use of pencil and paper in class. After following the plan he enthusiastically reported, "I hadn't the slightest difficulty in getting their attention, and I'm going to try that plan again." Similar testimonies might be multiplied, but sufficient has been said to prove that the blackboard is a valuable asset to the teacher.

How shall we use the blackboard? Shall we write a series of outlines, or draw a number of diagrams before the students come to class? This would produce the very opposite result from that intended, for two reasons: first, the students would be so busy scanning the artistic work that they would pay little attention to the teacher's words; second, such preparation would eliminate the elements of newness and surprise that are so necessary in stimulating curiosity. The use of the blackboard should be free and spontaneous, the teacher illustrating the truths as he utters them. For example, the lesson is the story of

Jesus' interview with the Samaritan woman. The teacher reads, "And He must needs go through Samaria." He moves toward the blackboard, and speaking very slowly, says, "The Jews were so prejudiced against the Samaritans (meanwhile he quickly draws a rough sketch of Palestine, indicating Judea, Samaria and Galilee) because of an old quarrel, that no Jew would go through Samaria (indicates); he would go around it (indicates). But Jesus knew no prejudice; all people looked alike to Him. Therefore He left Jerusalem (indicates) and passed through the land (indicates) that the Jews considered unclean." Notice the value of all this to the understanding of the lesson; the students have been *hearing and seeing* the truth at the same time. And the fact that the teacher illustrates as he talks stimulates the student's curiosity, because something new is happening all the time.

Again, suppose the teacher is about to state a brief, catchy outline: he says to the class, "Now, boys, that rich farmer about whom Jesus spoke (Luke 12: 13-22) made three big mistakes that I want everyone of you to avoid. Watch! I am going to write them on the board. And with every eye fixed upon the board the teacher writes:

1. HE MISTOOK HIMSELF FOR GOD.

2. HE MISTOOK HIS BODY FOR HIS SOUL.

3. HE MISTOOK TIME FOR ETERNITY.

The class will be much more likely to be interested and to remember the outline than if the teacher had simply stated it. Then too, it will be easier to hold their attention while enlarging upon these three points if he constantly points to the words on the board. In fact, so effective is blackboard drawing in creating interest that one writer has actually declared that one could hold the attention of an audience by simply stepping to the blackboard and standing there, chalk in hand, while speaking.

May we suggest another method of using the blackboard. The teacher reads, "And Jesus went into the Temple of God, and cast out all them that sold and bought in the temple, and overthrew the tables of the money-changers, and the seats of them that sold doves. "Now boys," says the teacher, "let's board the Holy Land Express and visit the temple in Jerusalem. Imagine an immense building, about a hundred feet high and nine hundred fifty feet square, made of pure white stone and pierced by gates of burnished brass about sixty-five feet high; imagine some parts covered with gold and jewels, and think of the sun shining on that building, which was situated on the top of a hill. A glorious sight, was it not? Now let's make a plan of the temple so that we may be able to locate the place where Jesus found those peddlers who were making the holy place hideous with their yells. Here are the boundaries of the Temple (draws a large square). Let's mark off the different courts. This line I'm now drawing bounds the court of the Gentiles, beyond which Gentiles could not pass; this space I am making is the court of the women, beyond which women were forbidden to pass; this is the court of Israel for the men; over here (still drawing) lies the court of the priests; here is the great altar of sacrifice, etc. Now, boys, it was in this place (making a cross), the court of the Gentiles, that the money-changers and merchants were carrying on their business. A poor example to those strangers, wasn't it! etc."

The blackboard may be used for writing certain words that drive home a lesson. Perhaps the teacher is speaking as follows: "The best way to get rid of a habit is not to start it, for if it is once contracted it is difficult to get rid of it. Why, even the *word* "habit" is hard to get rid of. Watch! I am going to write it on the board."

HABIT

Take off the "H" and you have

ABIT

Take off the "A" and you still have a

BIT

Take off the "B" and you still have

IT

Let us take another example. The third chapter of Genesis is under discussion. The teacher proceeds: "Anyone who has gone through the world with his eyes open knows that it is a place where evil abounds. And the great question has been, and still is, "Where did evil come from? How did sin enter into this world?" Moving toward the blackboard the teacher writes the word

EVIL

and remarks, "We get the Bible answer by spelling the word as follows:

D- EVIL

The blackboard may prove useful in teaching new

or difficult words to the class. For example: "Now, I think we all know what being *born again* means. There is a rather long name that is sometimes used to describe this experience (he moves toward the blackboard), and since you may hear a preacher use it, or you may read it in some book, I want you to remember it. Here it is":

REGENERATION

Only a few examples of what may be done have been given; in reality, there is no limit to what may be accomplished with the use of the blackboard. How often shall the blackboard be used? As often as possible, for the more the students are enabled to *see* the lesson the greater will be their interest, and the longer they will retain the lesson.

An interesting "Boy's eye-view" of the value of the blackboard comes to us from one who was well acquainted with Sunday School work. He tells of one boy who said, "I forget what the superintendent said our lesson is for, but I bet I'll never forget the sentence I saw on the blackboard."

OBJECTS

Objects have a twofold value: first, they appeal to the senses, thus stimulating interest; second, they have an educational value in that they make more real the subject that may be under consideration in the class. Objects are of two kinds: those that reproduce something that actually exists, and those that simply symbolize or suggest some spiritual truth.

The following are examples of symbolic objects:

1. The teacher is desirous of impressing the class with the importance of unity. He brings to class a

bundle of sticks, which he carefully hides until he is ready to use (a wise precaution). Declaring that there is unity in strength, he brings forth the bundle of sticks, and tells the students to watch him. He then attempts to break the bundle across his knee, but fails. He works hard, strains, and fails again. Finally, after a moment's thought he cuts the cord that binds them and breaks them across his knee one at a time. Such an illustration speaks for itself.

2. A lily and a bulb may be appropriately used to illustrate the resurrection.

3. In order to warn the class against evil influences the teacher may bring to class a charred stick; handle it, show his blackened hands, and ask, "Can we handle charred wood without soiling our hands? And can we associate with evil companions without becoming evil?"

4. The scars left by sin may be illustrated by driving nails into a board, each nail representing a sin. The nails may then be removed, representing repentance and forgiveness. Calling attention to the fact that though the nails are gone the holes still remain, the teacher could explain that sins, though forgiven, may leave their marks upon our lives. Therefore it is wise to take no chances.

5. In illustrating the force of habit the teacher may bind a student's wrists together with a thread. The student breaks it easily, of course. It may then be bound around twice, three times, and even four times, and still be broken. So the teacher binds it around many times, until the student can no longer break the threads. "In this way," explains the teacher,

"little sins committed again and again become big sins, and make slaves of us."

The following are examples of objects that represent actual, tangible things: a model of the Tabernacle in the Wilderness or of Solomon's Temple; a model of a house in the time of Christ; a small model of the scrolls of the law, used in the synagogue; Roman and Greek coins, etc.

In this same class we might mention good pictures, which are also valuable as a means of interesting the pupils, making Bible scenes real and inspiring them with the beauty of spiritual truths.

A word of caution is in order when speaking of objects. It is possible to spoil a class of children with them so that they will be constantly demanding something spectacular. As an extreme instance, a teacher undertaking to illustrate the falling stars preceding the coming of Christ might have the children continually asking for "more fireworks." This word of warning does not apply to blackboard drawing, however, for two reasons: first, the blackboard offers a natural way of presenting the lesson to the eye, while there is some danger that objects improperly selected may give the child a distorted idea of the truth; second, if the teacher has mastered the lesson he will not run short of material for blackboard illustrations, whereas it would be rather difficult to keep the class entertained every week with objects.

11

Impression and Expression

In Chapter 2 we learned that one of the fundamental principles of teaching is self-activity, or causing the student to express himself in some way. It is a fact that ten minutes of work done by the class is better than an hour's work done by the teacher. Amos R. Wells illustrates this truth as follows: One class of teachers stand before the students and shoot the rifle at the target. The other class *use the student* as the rifle and simply pull the trigger. As a matter of fact the students are already loaded with temptations, troubles, needs, curiosity, and information derived from the study of the lesson. By exciting curiosity and interest, the teacher supplies the powder and fulminating cap; by the use of skillful questions he pulls the trigger. This is simply a homely way of saying that the best teacher is the one who teaches the student to teach himself. It is evident, therefore, that there is no learning without mental activity on the part of the pupil. And in order to insure mental activity, the pupil must be led in some way to express its result.

There are two main steps in the learning process: first, *impression,* represented by the reading and study of the lesson and the teacher's remarks; second, *expression,* by which the pupil gives out the results of his own thinking or labor. It is expression that completes the learning process and puts the pupil in possession of the truth, for only what we give out is really our own. In teaching, impression should always be followed by expression. Let us consider three illustrations supporting this truth.

The principle is true in the spiritual realm. Wise spiritual leaders urge young converts to express their recent spiritual experience in some form of service —testimony, personal work, etc. Why? Because life that is not expressed dies. If we do not use we lose. "If ye *know* these things," declared Jesus, "happy are ye if ye *do* them."

Teachers themselves have experienced the truth that we really learn by doing. A Sunday School teacher works hard over his material, and comes to class with heart and mind stocked with truth and emotion. But he does not really learn the lesson until after he has taught, or expressed it. For in the very act of teaching, truths that may have been vague or shapeless have taken definite form as they have passed from mind to mind; facts that seemed rather dry have been ignited with Divine fire as they have passed from heart to heart. And very often the teacher leaves the class, tingling with the power of the truth that he has learned while teaching others.

Two boys set themselves, let us say, to the study of the plans and specifications of the Tabernacle as set forth in Exodus 25 to 40. One boy reads the chapters and masters them intellectually. The other studies the same chapters and then constructs a model of the Tabernacle. Which of the two will know more about the Tabernacle, and which one will really possess that knowledge? The one who constructed the Tabernacle, of course; for only that which we create by our own activity do we really possess. And in a general sense, whenever the pupil expresses himself in any way concerning the lesson, he is engaged in creative activity.

How may the pupils express themselves? Each department of the Sunday School has its forms of expression. With Beginners it is in the form of play or some physical activity; with Primaries it is in the form of drawing with crayons or chalk, cutting silhouettes, or acting out the story; the Juniors and Intermediates will find their outlet in the way of handwork, written work, construction of objects, and memory work; in the higher departments assignments and research work will provide the means of self-expression.

In our next chapter we shall discuss one of the most effective means of securing expression; namely, the asking of questions.

12

Teaching by Questions

Many hundreds of years ago a wise man said, "A shrewd question is the half of knowledge." That statement holds true today; good questions make good teaching, and a good questioner is generally a good teacher. In fact, the question is the teacher's most clear-cut and effective tool. Questions are valuable because they cause the students to express themselves, and thus complete the process of learning. The student may have studied the lesson and heard it explained by the teacher. It has made an impression. His mind is filled with thoughts, feelings, and problems connected with that impression. But these ideas are not definitely formed in his mind—they are vague and in disorder. The teacher's use of a good question sets the wheels of the pupil's mind to working. It causes him to express himself, and in this self-expression, what he has studied becomes clear; fog and confusion are banished; he says to himself, "Well, that is certainly clear to me now; why didn't I think of all that before?" He is surprised and delighted at what has come forth from his own mind.

But in order to produce this effect the questions must be carefully prepared and skillfully used. We shall therefore consider the main purposes in the use of questions, and give some rules for accomplishing those purposes.

Questions are used to accomplish the following results:

    1. Develop the lesson.
    2. Clarify the lesson.
    3. Make the student think.
    4. Emphasize the important truths.
    5. Keep the class occupied.

1. DEVELOP THE LESSON

Since the lesson should be taught in an orderly manner, questions should be prepared in a logical order. The questions in the quarterly are for the benefit of the teacher, rather than that of the scholar. Begin with easy questions in order to encourage the pupil.

2. CLARIFY THE LESSON

If the questions are to make the meaning of the lesson clear they should not be such as to confuse the students, as do the following types of questions:

Compound questions. For example, "Who said what, and why did he say it when he was nearly drowned in the Sea of Galilee? (See Matt. 14:28). There are in reality three questions here: (1) Who spoke up at this point? (2) What did he say? (3) Why did he say it?

Questions containing big words. One of the foundation principles of teaching is that truth must be adapted to the understanding of the pupil. Therefore a group of boys should not be addressed with a question like the following: "Did the apostasy of Judas imply any premeditation on his part?" The Bible was written in the language of the common people; and the Lord said, "Feed my *sheep*," not, "Feed my giraffes."

Questions that admit of more than one meaning. A teacher once asked a child, "What must be done before our sins can be forgiven?" The child answered, "We must sin first." And the answer was correct in the sense that the question was understood. A better way of asking the question would have been as follows: "After we have sinned, what must we do in order to be forgiven?" Another question that might receive several answers is, "Who was Pilate?" A Roman; a governor; the one who condemned Jesus to be crucified; a judge. This question might be clarified by asking: "What was Pilate's nationality? his official position? his attitude toward Jesus? his attitude toward the Jewish leaders?

Vague questions such as, "What happens when we sin?" could be made more definite by asking, "What is the effect upon the conscience when a person sins?"

Questions that raise questions, like the following: "Why was Paul the apostle out of God's will in going to Jerusalem, following his third missionary journey?" That would raise the question, "But *was* he out of God's will?"

Long-winded questions; such, for example, as those long German sentences in which, as one writer has said, one can travel all day without changing cars. Of this type of question the following is an example: "Do you think that in the days of Herod the Great, a cruel, jealous king, who was always suspicious that someone was aspiring to the throne (in fact he murdered his own wife and son) that it would have been safe for anyone to announce the birth of a king (especially since they had made no secret of it, but had spread the news over the entire city) and expose themselves and the Divine Child to the cruelty of this man, who was so cruel that, knowing the Jews would rejoice at the news of his death, ordered a number of prominent men to be put into prison in Jericho and to be killed after his death, so that the nation would have occasion to mourn his death?" This is not a question—it is a lecture.

To sum up: questions should not mystify, but should be clear and understandable. They should not obscure the subject, but throw some light on the ground to be covered. Not that they should reveal the answer, and so save the pupil the trouble of thinking; but the pupils should at least know what the questions mean.

3. MAKE THE STUDENT THINK

"Never tell a scholar what you can make the scholar tell you," is an old teaching maxim. In other words, "Give as little information as possible and require as much information as possible." The purpose of recitation is not to enable the teacher to pull out of the student's mouth the identical words and ideas that he has put into his ears. When a farmer takes his grain to mill he does not expect it to be returned to him in the same condition in which he brought it; he expects to find it ground. The teacher gives out the grain of truth, that it may pass through the mill of the student's thinking and come out, ground, so to speak.

In order to be sure that the student is really thinking, it is best to avoid the following types of questions:

Questions that suggest the answer. For example, the question, "What should people confess?" really answers itself.

Questions that may be answered by yes or no. Such answers may be simply a matter of guesswork. In any case, they give no evidence that the student has done any real thinking. Marion Lawrance tells us, "Scholars are quite ready to give the answer which they know the teacher expects, until they run up against a wall and make themselves ridiculous. For example, in my own school on one occasion, our pastor tried this experiment. He questioned the whole school quite rapidly in the following manner: "Scholars, do you think we ought to be regular in attendance?" "Yes, sir." "Do you think we ought to be on time every Sunday morning?" "Yes, sir." "Do you think we ought to study our lessons at home?" "Yes, sir." Do you think we ought to bring an offering every Sunday?" "Yes, sir." *"Do you think I ought to stop talking to you now?"* "Yes, sir."

Questions asked and answered in the identical words of the lesson. The student should be required to answer in his own language, for it is possible for him to know the words of an answer without having the slightest idea as to its meaning. Sir Joshua Fitch (a noted educator), in his book, *The Art of Questioning,* even insists that the pupil do not use the language of Scripture in his answer, but state the answer in his own words. He gives the following illustration taken from Luke 10:30.

> Who is this parable about? *A certain man.*
> Where did he go from? *Jerusalem.*
> Where to? *Jericho.*

What sort of people did he fall among? *Thieves.*
What did they do with his raiment? *Stripped him of it.*
What did they do with the man himself? *Wounded him.*
In what state did they leave him? *Half dead.*

"Observe here that the teacher has covered the whole area of the narrative and proposed a question on every fact; so far he has done well.

"But notice that every question was proposed as nearly as possible in the words of the book, and required for its answer one (generally *but* one) of those words. Now it is very easy for a boy or girl, while the echoes of the Bible narrative just read still linger in the ear, to answer every such question by rote merely, with scarcely any effort of memory, and no effort of thought whatever.

Let us go over the same subject again, first introducing it by one or two preliminary questions; for example:

Who used these words? To whom were they spoken? Why were they uttered? Repeat the question which the lawyer asked.

What is the parable about? *A man who went on a journey.* What do you call a man who goes on a journey? *A traveler.* In what country was the man traveling? *Judea.* Let us trace his route on the map. In what direction was he traveling? *Eastward.*

Through what kind of country? (Teacher to supply facts about its physical features.)

What should you suppose was the state of the country at that time? *Thinly populated; road unfrequented.*

How do you know that? *Because he fell among thieves.* Give another word for thieves. *Robbers.*

How did the robbers treat this traveler? *They stripped him of his clothes.*

What else did they do? *Wounded him.*

Explain that word. *Injured him, hurt him very much.*

How do you know from the text that he was much hurt? *They left him half dead. They almost killed him.*

"Now observe here that the aim has been two-fold. First, not to suggest the answer by the form of question. Hence the children have been made to interpret the Biblical language by that of ordinary life. Second, not to be satisfied with single words as answers, especially with the particular word which is contained in the narrative itself, but always to translate it into one more familiar."

The principle of requiring the pupil to use his own words when reciting is further illustrated by the following instance, related by W. P. Spilman, in which a rough little chap tells the lesson story in his own words.

"It was in the Rocky Mountains of Wyoming, several miles north of Laramie. A visitor was called on to teach a class of boys whose ages varied from seven to ten. The lesson of the Sunday before was about the Good Samaritan.

"Now," said the teacher, "which of you boys can tell me about the lesson for last Sunday?" Several hands went up. One boy was selected. "Tell all you know about it," said the teacher.

"Well, sir," said the boy, "the lesson for last Sunday was 'bout the hold-up in the Jericho Canyon. Dere was a man traveling, and a gang o' toughs got up wid 'im and welted him one and mighty nigh killed him. Then they touched him for his wad and scooted. Here come along a doctor. He said, 'Ugh, dat ain't none o' my medicine,' and went on. Here come along a preacher. He look at de fellow and say, 'Dat case ain't in my parish,' an' he went on. Den here come along a cowboy on his broncho. He jump off an' say, 'Hello, dis fellow is hurt.' Den he put him on de broncho an' carry 'im to de roadhouse an' say to the fellow, 'Now here, dis fellow got into it down yonder in de canyon and got hurt. You take care of 'im. He's my pal, and here's my wad, and if you're out anything when I come back from de ranch, I'll square it.' "

We are aware that the language in which this parable was told is decidedly crude, but who can doubt that the little fellow had grasped the lesson?

Note. The teacher should be careful not to discourage pupils by rejecting an answer that may be imperfect or incomplete, but should tactfully give credit for it, and correct it. If the pupil makes some errors while reciting, it is best to permit him to continue without interruption, for the main purpose in asking a question is not merely to get an accurate statement, but to lead the student to express himself and to understand the truth. And even if the answer is wrong, it accomplishes an important service, in that it enables the teacher to correct some misconception in the student's mind.

4. IMPORTANCE

The student should not be questioned concerning minor and non-essential details. "To ask a question emphasizes the thing asked," writes Dr. Weigle, "for it becomes the center of thought for the moment. It gets impressed upon the student's mind and acquires dignity and importance in his eyes." For example, if the teacher should ask, "To what kind of closet did Jesus refer—a clothes closet or a private room?" and should spend five minutes or more discussing the matter, it would be wasting too much time on a minor detail; for the important point in the lesson is not the *place,* but the *manner* of prayer.

Question and answer should form two important parts of a truth that is worth while remembering. For example, the teacher asks, "As Peter thoughtfully watched the retreating figure of the rich young ruler, what question did he ask?" (Matt. 19:27-29). The student will reason as follows: "What has the *rich young ruler* to do with Peter's question? I see! Peter was comparing himself with this rich young man who had refused to give up all for Christ and that's why he asked, 'Behold, *we* have left all and followed Thee; what shall *we* have therefore?'" Let us take another example: "What did Jesus do when He perceived that the apostles would not perform the hospitable duty of washing one another's feet?" The student will say to himself, "Well, I see new light on that subject. Each one thought he was too 'big' to wash the feet of his brother, so the Leader humbled Himself to put them to shame."

The above are examples of questions that teach and that result in the combination of a good question and a good answer.

5. KEEP THE CLASS OCCUPIED

In asking questions the entire class should be kept in mind rather than any individual; the aim of the teacher should be to keep everyone interested and at work. In this regard the following suggestions may prove helpful.

Avoid partiality. An experienced teacher tells us, "There are certain 'smarties' that are anxious to show off by answering every question the teacher puts. This should not be permitted. There are those who can answer only the simplest questions. Give the simple questions, especially at first, and give the hardest questions to the best scholars. It is altogether wrong to show favoritism in the answering of questions; wrong to those who answer and wrong to those who are relieved of the responsibility."

Avoid repeating the question for the sake of an inattentive pupil. It is not meet that the class's time should be wasted because of one careless pupil. And the teacher's passing on quickly to some other pupil will be a gentle rebuke and reminder to the inattentive one.

Call upon the same pupil more than once. This will keep the pupil from thinking that after answering one question his work for the entire period is over.

Keep after the pupil who fails to answer. If his failure is due to neglect of study it will remind him of his responsibility; if it is due to lack of ability the teacher's patience will be an encouragement to him.

Address the question to the entire class. If the teacher says, "Now, Johnny Jones, I want you to answer this question," other members of the class may say to themselves, "Well, that's Johnny's question," and will let him do the thinking. In order to secure the attention of the entire class, before asking a question one might say, "Listen closely, boys, for I have an important question for you." Having aroused their interest and stated the question, the teacher may then choose one student and say, "All right, Jimmie, you may answer this question." Why choose Jimmie? Because he is the least attentive boy in the class. If he begins to realize that his inattention is drawing fire in the form of a question he will very likely pay attention to avoid "losing face" before the entire class.

13

Story Telling

It has been well said that "of all things that a teacher should know the most important without exception is to be able to tell a story." The reason for this statement is that story-telling is one of the most vital, interesting, and effective ways of presenting spiritual truth. And "Truth. convincingly portrayed, is the mightiest force the world has ever known," declares one teacher who has had years of experience in story-telling. This is unquestionably true in regard to children. The influences during the first five or six years of a child's life are more potent in shaping ideals and attitudes than at any other time; and by means of well-told stories the interests, desires, and emotions of the child may be made to respond to that which is good and beautiful and to react against that which is evil and ugly. Gripped by the interest of the story, children, whether good or bad, are changed into reverent listeners, and as their sympathies and dislikes are aroused by the portrayal of various scenes and characters, they may be led to love righteousness and to hate sin, just as surely as they may be taught the multiplication table. In all lands and in all ages great has been the power of the story to mold character, impress ideals, create attitudes, and to teach standards. Consequently, the skillful telling of the inspired stories of the Bible is the mightiest force in the world for influencing people for God and righteousness.

Grown-ups, too, respond to the appeal of the story. All over our land the printing presses are turning out novels by the tens of thousands in response to a constant demand. Some of these stories have value, some are worthless, and others positively harmful. But the very demand is proof that people like stories; this being the case, the wise teacher will use the story for the highest of purposes—that of conveying spiritual truth. It is invaluable as a means of securing attention. A congregation may become listless and sleepy under a doctrinal discussion, but let the preacher arrest the flow of exposition, and begin to tell a story, and the half slumbering listeners will look up with open eyes and open mouth.

WHAT IS A STORY?

It has been defined as a "connected narrative of that which has occurred; a description of past events." But the kind of story we have in mind for Sunday School work is more than that, for it is possible, for example, to state the fact that the milk was stolen from the front porch without "sending a group of children into a quiver of expectancy." The story which has teaching value must *stir the emotions,* grip the interest, and thus stamp the truth upon mind and heart. It is "a picture that arouses intense interest and feeling." A good way to define the kind of story that has teaching value is to state what it accomplishes. A good story—

1. Arouses interest.
2. Inspires sympathy.

3. Produces reality.
4. Influences conduct.

1. *The story arouses interest by touching the emotions.* The chief value of the story lies in its power to create interest and to produce enjoyment. The listener is gripped by the characters and the scenes, and his feelings touched by what is done and said; meanwhile, however, the practical lessons represented by those characters and scenes are being stamped upon his mind and heart. Thus the value of the story is indirect; for while the pupil is held in a spell of interest, and is watching the development of the plot, either admiring or disliking the person described, the moral lesson slips in through the back door of the mind, so to speak, and before the pupil knows it, he is influenced.

Nathan used this method to bring home to David's conscience the guilt of his double crime. Read 2 Sam. 12:1-7. The prophet did not begin by administering a direct rebuke, for quite likely the king had already fortified himself with a barrier of plausible excuses and arguments. But Nathan employed the indirect method and gained the king's attention and aroused his interest by telling him a story. With the seeming intention of bringing before David a judicial case, he recounted the following incident:

There were two men in one city; the one rich, and the other poor. The rich man had exceeding many flocks and herds: but the poor man had nothing, save one little ewe lamb, which he had bought and nourished up: and it grew up together with him, and with his children; it did eat of his own meat, and drank of his own cup, and lay in his bosom, and was unto him as a daughter. And there came a traveller unto the rich man, and he spared to take of his own flock and of his own herd, to dress for the wayfaring man that was come unto him; but took the poor man's lamb, and dressed it for the man that was come to him.

Notice what happened. David's interest was immediately aroused and his heart was stirred. For the poor man who had been robbed of his pet he felt a tender pity that must have brought tears to his eyes; against the heartless rich man he felt a burning sense of indignation that blazed forth in the words, "As the Lord liveth, the man that hath done this thing shall surely die: and he shall restore the lamb fourfold, because he did this thing and because he had no pity."

Up to this point the king had not realized that the story described his own sin. He was as yet unaware of the fact that he felt pity for the man he himself had wronged, that his fiery anger was really directed against himself, and that he had pronounced his own condemnation. *The story had truly done its work;* and it required but four words to apply the lesson to David's conscience and bring him down to the dust of penitence: "Thou art the man!"

2. By arousing interest the story begets sympathy. Stories influence human action because they touch the heart and make people *feel* with the characters whose acts make the story. The listener is moved to admiration for righteousness, to approval for the merciful, to loathing for sin. For the moment the pupil forgets himself, and begins to experience, think, and feel with the characters of the story. The human heart is filled with emotions; by means of the stories of the Bible these emotions may be enlisted on the side of God and righteousness and stirred against the devil and unrighteousness.

One day the Lord Jesus confronted the Jewish leaders, men who were descendants of those who stoned the prophets and whose hearts were filled with hatred and murder against their Messiah. In order to make them *feel* that this was the case, and thus cause them unconsciously to pronounce their own condemnation, He told the following story in Matt. 21:33-40:

There was a certain householder, which planted a vineyard, and hedged it round about, and digged a winepress in it, and built a tower, and let it out to husbandmen, and went into a far country: and when the time of the fruit drew near, he sent his servants to the husbandmen, that they might receive the fruits of it.

And the husbandmen took his servants, and beat one, and killed another, and stoned another. Again, he sent other servants more than the first: and they did unto them likewise. But last of all he sent unto them his son, saying, 'They will reverence my son.' But when the husbandmen saw the son, they said among themselves, 'This is the heir; come, let us kill him, and let us seize on his inheritance.' And they caught him, and cast him out of the vineyard, and slew him. When the Lord therefore of the vineyard cometh, what will he do unto those husbandmen?

Their interest in the story became so great that for a moment they forgot their animosity, and listened intently; but more than that, they *felt* with the characters. We may imagine one of the priests, himself a landowner, saying to himself, "The ungrateful rascals—not only refusing to pay the rent, but mistreating and murdering the collectors. I never would have borne so long with those wicked tenants as that long-suffering landlord did. The first manifestation of violence would have brought a detachment of Roman soldiers to that farm, and a good scourging and a sojourn in a dungeon would have taught those farmers better manners." Again, we may imagine the thoughts of one of the Pharisees: "Can a worse example of godless violation of solemn obligation be imagined than this one! Surely Divine justice would demand the death of those rogues and murderers!" That they were moved is indicated by their answer to Christ's question in verse 41, "They (the Jewish leaders) say unto Him (Jesus), 'He will miserably destroy those wicked men, and will let out his vineyard unto other husbandmen, which shall render him the fruits in their season.'" In reality, they had pronounced their own condemnation, and it required but a few additional words to make them see it. "Therefore I say unto you the kingdom of God (symbolized by the vineyard) shall be taken from you (religious leaders) and given to a nation (a new chosen nation, the church) bringing forth the fruits thereof." Without their realizing it, those religious leaders had been made to *feel* that they, the descendants of the persecutors of the prophets, were, in intention, the murderers of the Messiah, God's Son.

If the telling of a story could affect those who were enemies of Christ, how much more will it stir and influence those, especially children, whose hearts are responsive to Him!

3. *By arousing sympathy the story produces reality.* Stories make spiritual teaching real because they exhibit spiritual and moral principles *in action.* One day a lawyer asked Jesus the question, "Who is my neighbor?" Reading between the lines we are inclined to believe that this teacher of the law had perhaps been guilty of some unneighborly conduct toward one of

another nationality or class, for behind his question was the desire to "justify himself." Of course, Jesus might have answered the question in a few words, telling the man that the very question implied a lack of the neighborly spirit. But, skillful Teacher that He was, He used a story, The Good Samaritan, to demonstrate the neighborly and unneighborly spirit *in action*. In the man who was brutally beaten by thieves the lawyer saw a vivid picture of needy humanity, and in the callous indifference of priest and Levite he must have seen his own lack of compassion, while in the kindly Samaritan he saw the life-like portrait of a real neighbor. That Samaritan, who represented neighborliness in action, was the answer to the lawyer's question. And he understood, for when Jesus asked, "Which now of these three, thinkest thou, was neighbour unto him that fell among the thieves?" he answered, "He that shewed mercy on him." He had received more than an intellectual understanding of the subject; he had *felt* and *seen* the kind of man he should be.

4. *By inspiring reality the story influences conduct.* When truths are made real by being emphasized in the characters of a story, there results a feeling of reality which tends to cause those truths to function in the behavior of the pupil. As his emotions are moved to feel respect or contempt for the actions of individuals mentioned in a story, those actions are bound to sway him. Observing that the lawyer was moved by the story of the Good Samaritan, the Lord Jesus said, "Go, and *do* thou likewise."

HOW TO TELL A STORY

In order to tell a story effectively one must—
Know it.
See it.
Feel it.

The teacher must know the story. The teacher cannot clearly visualize the scenes of a story and be able to command a ready flow of words with which to paint a vivid word-picture upon the canvas of the student's eye without having first completely mastered the substance of the story. In mastering a story the following suggestions may be found useful:

Prepare and practice the story. This will involve work; the inspiration will come later when the teacher faces the class. The story need not be memorized, word for word, but it is essential that the story-teller have a clear mental picture of every scene, main characters, customs, and conversation.

Simplify the story by the elimination of unnecessary details, unimportant incidents and minor characters, that may hinder the smooth and orderly development of the main plot or incident. Miss Katherine Dunlap Cather, who has told a great many stories to children, has given us the following example of a well-told Bible story:

HOW DAVID USED HIS HARP

Among the sunny hills of Bethlehem, David, the shepherd boy, tended his sheep. He was a good shepherd, leading the flocks to green pastures and still waters, and watching all the while that no harm came to them. Sometimes he sang songs as he followed them over the slopes, and sometimes as he sang he played on a harp and made music that sounded far over the hills.

Now, it happened that in the same country there lived

a king whose name was Saul. King Saul was unhappy. He had been sick a long, long time, and nothing the doctors and wise men of the land could do had made him feel any better. He had forgotten how to smile, and because he had sad, gloomy thoughts all the while, deep wrinkles came into his face.

One day some wise men began to wonder if music might make him happy and well again. They told their thoughts to the king, and he said, "Find a man who can play on the harp and bring him to me."

"There is a shepherd of Bethlehem who is skillful in playing," one of them said. "He is strong and kind and very fair to look upon. He is the son of Jesse and is called David."

A messenger was sent to seek him, and as David wandered here and there with the white flocks, petting the gentle ewes and watching that the lambs did not stray into dangerous places, word came that he should go to the king. His father gave him a present of bread and other good things to lay before King Saul. And then sent him on his way.

When he came into the presence of the King he began to play. He played a song that he made for the sheep at evening when shadows were darkening the hills and he took them to the fold. Then he played a tune that the crickets and the quails and the wild rabbits stopped to hear, and the songs the people sang as they cut the grain and made merry at weddings. And the music pleased King Saul so much that he began to smile. He forgot the sad thoughts and felt better, and very soon he was well again. He was a very happy king now. And David was happy too. He was glad to think he had helped with his songs and his harp.

After that, whenever Saul was sick or in trouble, David played and sang for him and made him glad. And by and by he himself became king of Israel, and wrote for us many beautiful psalms.

In relating a story the incidents should be kept in logical order, for nothing so spoils a story as for the narrator to pause and say, "Oh, I forgot to tell you that . . ." An outline will be of assistance in remembering the order of events. For an example, let us notice carefully the following outline of the story of the Flood, as given by Miss Cather:

A race of mighty men; all but Noah grew wicked as they grew in strength.

God grieved by wickedness; determines to destroy; bids Noah build ark.

Building of the ark; Noah's family go into ark; animals also.

The flood.

The abating of the storm; Noah sends forth raven and dove; dove returns.

Sends out second time; returns with olive leaf.

Noah removes covering of ark; goes forth with family and animals.

Builds altar unto the Lord.

As far as possible, keep in mind the exact conversations and words used by the different characters, for it is better to use the first person than the third. Read the story of Jesus' turning the water into wine, and notice how flat it would sound if all direct conversation were eliminated and the indirect form used. For example, compare the following statements: "His mother told the servants to do whatever He said unto them"; and, "His mother said to the servants, 'Whatsoever He saith unto you, do it.'"

The teacher should see the story. The story must be not only in the memory but also in the imagination of the teacher, for only so can it be made to stir the imaginations of others. For example, the subject of the lesson is the story of Zacchaeus. While the teacher is speaking, the pupils forget that they are in the United States, and they find themselves on the hot, dusty roads of Palestine. As they walk along, with the hot sun beating down upon them, they are attracted by a large crowd, wending its way through Jericho. Approaching the crowd, they catch glimpses of various classes of people—the haughty Sadducee, dressed in white, looking on with contempt; the sanctimonious Pharisee, with prayer-shawl and phylacteries, watching for something to criticize; the ragged beggar shuffling along, pleading for alms; the publican, with his crafty, shifting glances; a Roman soldier in glistening armor. In the midst of the crowd is Jesus, talking with His disciples, and surrounded by a group of enthusiasts who think that He goes to Jerusalem to set up His kingdom. Then, as the story continues, the attention of the pupils is drawn to a little man named Zacchæus, standing on tip-toe, and dashing from one point to another in a vain attempt to see the great Rabbi. Jostled and pushed about by a crowd which resents the forwardness of that "apostate publican," Zacchæus suddenly runs ahead, nimbly climbs a tree, and from this vantage point looks down with eager eyes upon the crowd below. At last he spies Jesus! But will Jesus see him?—and so on with the story. Thus the teacher proceeds to make his listeners see the various scenes and characters of the story—but he must see them first himself.

The teacher must feel the story. It is useless for a teacher to tell a story that he himself does not appreciate or enjoy. It is necessary for him to be thrilled and stirred by what he sees, so that "the overflow from one pulsing heart may water the dry places in other hearts." His own imagination and emotions must be aroused if he would arouse the imaginations of others to see and feel the scenes for themselves. And when the teacher himself is moved by the scenes and characters of the story he is telling he need not worry about appropriate gestures, expressions, or eloquence, for "out of the abundance of the heart the mouth speaketh."

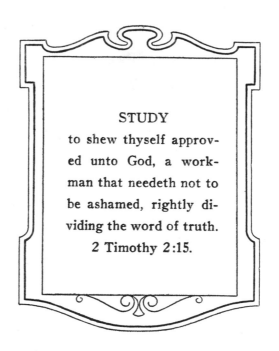

STUDY

to shew thyself approved unto God, a workman that needeth not to be ashamed, rightly dividing the word of truth.

2 Timothy 2:15.